TEACHE

BECOMING A SECO

BECOMING A
SECONDARY HEADTEACHER

Julia Evetts

CASSELL

Cassell
Villiers House   387 Park Avenue South
41/47 Strand   New York
London WC2N 5JE   NY 10016-8810

First published 1994

British Library Cataloguing-in-Publication Data
A catalogue record for this book is available from the British Library.

ISBN   0-304-32672-0 (hardback)
       0-304-32670-4 (paperback)

Typeset by Colset Pte Ltd, Singapore
Printed and bound in Great Britain by Redwood Books, Trowbridge, Wiltshire

Contents

Foreword

In Britain and Australia, they call it teaching. In the United States and Canada, they call it instruction. Whatever terms we use, we have come to realize in recent years that the teacher is the ultimate key to educational change and school improvement. The restructuring of schools, the composition of national and provincial curricula, the development of benchmark assessments − all these things are of little value if they do not take the teacher into account. Teachers do not merely deliver the curriculum; they develop, define it and reinterpret it. It is what teachers think, what teachers believe and what teachers do at the level of the classroom that ultimately shapes the kind of learning that young people receive. Growing appreciation of this fact is placing working with teachers and understanding teaching at the top of our research and improvement agendas.

For some reformers, improving teaching is mainly a matter of developing better teaching methods, of improving instruction. Training teachers in new classroom management skills, in active learning, co-operative learning, one-to-one counselling and the like, is the main priority. These things are important, but we are also increasingly coming to understand that developing teachers and improving their teaching involves more than giving them new tricks. We are beginning to recognize that, for teachers, what goes on inside the classroom is closely related to what goes on outside it. The quality, range and flexibility of teachers' classroom work are closely tied up with their professional growth − with the way that they develop as people and as professionals.

Teachers teach in the way they do not just because of the skills they have or have not learned. Their approach is also grounded in their backgrounds, their biographies, in the kinds of teachers they have become. Their careers − their hopes and dreams, their opportunities and aspirations, or the frustration of these things − are also important for teachers' commitment, enthusiasm and morale. So too are relationships with their colleagues − either as supportive communities who work together in pursuit of common goals and continuous improvement, or as individuals working in isolation, with the insecurities that sometimes brings.

As we are coming to understand these wider aspects of teaching and teacher development, we are also beginning to recognize that much more than pedagogy, instruction or teaching method is at stake. Teachers' development; their careers relations with their colleagues; the conditions of status, reward and leadership under which they work − all these affect the quality of what they do in the classroom.

This international series, Teacher Development, brings together some of the best current research and writing on these aspects of teachers' lives and work. The books in the series seek to understand the wider dimensions of teachers' work, the depth of teachers' knowledge and the resources of biography and experience on which it draws, the ways that teachers' work roles and responsibilities are changing as we restructure our schools, and so forth. In this sense, the books in the series are written for those who are involved in research on teaching, those who work in initial and in-service teacher education, those who lead and administer teachers, those who work with teachers and, not least, teachers themselves.

Although research in recent years had told us a lot about teachers' lives and careers and their implications for teacher development, the lives and careers of headteachers or principals and their implications for leadership development are understood not nearly so well. The once predictable pathways of headteacher's and school principals' careers are in many ways being redrawn. More women are becoming school leaders, bringing different assumptions and orientations with them to the task of leadership than their male predecessors. The ethos of school leadership is also changing with moves towards greater school self-management. This kind of self-governing freedom can be problematic for those who were attracted to headship for other reasons, and attracts different kinds of leaders to take their place. The lives and careers of headteachers or principals have long been a suitable case for investigation, but the changing nature of school leadership poses a particularly pressing reason why our understanding of it should be subject to fundamental review.

Julia Evetts's books shows, through intimate and intensive investigation, what the lives and careers of headteachers today are like; how they vary between leaders of different generations; how they differ along gender lines and how they are being re-shaped in more managerial times. Evetts elucidates the crucial connections between headteachers' formal careers and their private lives — showing how intricately each is embedded in the other. She shows how teachers' careers are constructed through emotion and morality, as well as through the calculations of strategy.

This is a book that gets beneath and beyond the ideal worlds and simplistic fashions and prescriptions of management theory applied to schools. It opens up and takes readers inside headteachers' lives and careers. It portrays head-teaching straightforwardly in all its humanity, complexity and imperfection. Understand a life and you are close to understanding the work of the person who lives it. Headteachers' lives deserve such understanding, not least among headteachers themselves. In its compilation of cases and quotations, and in the analyses that flow from them, *Becoming a Secondary Headteacher* supplies a splendid mirror through which such reflection can take place.

Andy Hargreaves, Professor OISE
August 1994

Preface

This book examines the processes and procedures involved in developing a career in teaching and becoming a secondary headteacher in England. It makes use of career history data from a group of secondary headteachers from two local educational authorities in England in order to illustrate the topics discussed. The interrelationship of career structures, the constraints and determinants of career progress, and career action, i.e. the promotion experiences of individual headteachers, is a theme linking the discussions in the separate chapters. The issue of gender and headship is also a recurrent theme, since an exploration of gender differences in career and in experiences of headship was one of the objectives of my research. The book focuses on recent educational changes in Britain and considers change as the critical context in the construction of headteacher careers. The structural determinants of and constraints which limit careers and promotions to headteacher positions are very real, but career actions can alter structures just as career structures affect and constrain actions. This interrelationship of career determinants and experiences constitutes the theoretical background for the analysis of the processes involved in becoming a secondary headteacher.

Acknowledgements

A large number of people have helped me during the years in which the ideas and themes in this book have been developed. I would like to thank my colleagues in the School of Social Studies at the University of Nottingham for the discussions we have had about careers in teaching and in other professions. In particular l would like to thank Michael King for his encouragement and for his comments on the structure/action dimensions. Robert Burgess gave continuing support and Andy Hargreaves assisted in the early planning.

Particular thanks go to the secondary headteachers who gave of their time and shared their experiences. They cannot be named but without them this study would not exist. I hope I have done justice to their accounts and been able to reflect some of their concerns as well as the intricacies of their lives and careers. Any faults in the text are, of course, my own.

Linda Poxon typed all my work with great care and efficiency. Her willingness, speed and accuracy enable me to overcome the difficulties posed by a strain injury to my right hand and arm.

I would like to thank the following journals for permission to draw on previously published work: *British Journal of Sociology of Education*, 13 (1), 1992, for 'When promotion ladders seem to end'; *Educational Review*, 45 (1), 1993, for 'LMS and headship'; *Educational Studies*, 17 (3), 1991, for 'The experience of secondary headship'; *School Organisation*, 12 (1), 1992, for 'The organization of staff in secondary schools; and *Sociological Review*, 41 (2), 1993, for 'Careers and partnerships'.

Finally I would like to thank my husband, Dave, for his practical help and continuing support. His calmness is a source of great strength to me.

Julia Evetts
University of Nottingham

Introduction

RESEARCH ON HEADTEACHERS: THE BACKGROUND

Research on teachers and teaching has been profuse in sociology and in education. Research on headteachers and headship has been generally less frequent although there are notable exceptions. In North America, research on principals and school leadership has been very common (Wolcott, 1973; McCleary and Thomson, 1979; Blumberg and Greenfield, 1980; Greenfield, 1982). Such research has been intermittent in Britain, with an increase in the 1980s and, in recent years, a tremendous growth in the literature on the organization and management of schools. The growth in numbers of large comprehensive schools together with more recent developments, such as local management of schools (LMS), budgetary devolution and grant-maintained status for schools, have heightened awareness of the importance of management in educational establishments. The management literature has been both theoretical (for example, the Open University readers; see Bush, 1989), and practical in orientation (e.g. Lyons and Stenning, 1986; Adams, 1987). Only part of it has focused exclusively on headteachers since the growth in managerialism in schools has resulted in hierarchical management structures of senior and middle management. Changes to the headteacher's role have received attention (Peters, 1976; Earley and Weindling, 1987): the expansion of managerial and administrative tasks and the reduction in educational leadership being two aspects to have been documented (Morgan *et al.*, 1983; Evetts, 1991).

SOCIOLOGICAL RESEARCH: CHANGING MODELS 1950–90

Within the discipline of sociology, from the 1950s to the 1990s there have been important changes in the popularity of theoretical models and shifts in research methods. As they relate to research on teachers, these changes have been catalogued by Ball and Goodson (1985). In the 1950s and 1960s the focus was on 'role' (Stiles, 1957; Wilson, 1962), on 'professionalization' (Lieberman, 1956; Etzioni, 1969) and on statistical analyses of the characteristics of teachers and of their position in society (Tropp, 1957; Floud and Scott, 1961; Kelsall, 1963).

In the 1970s, according to Ball and Goodson, the emphasis shifted to the constraints on teachers' work. Some studies (Sharp and Green, 1975; Woods, 1979) focused on the societal and economic determinants of education and explained how constraints limited both the aims and the practice of teachers' work. The 1970s also saw a revival of the interactionist theoretical perspective in research in the sociology of education, which continued in the 1980s. This perspective emphasized individuals' construction of reality, stressing meaning, understanding and experience (Woods, 1983) and was used extensively in research on teachers and teachers' careers (Hammersley, 1977; Woods, 1980; Riseborough, 1981; Nias, 1984, 1985; Ball and Goodson, 1985; Sikes *et al.*, 1985). The effect of such research was to focus attention on the immediate practical problems of being a teacher and coping day by day in schools and classrooms. In the 1980s there were fruitful exchanges between interactionist approaches and researchers emphasizing the wider societal, economic and cultural constraints on teachers (Ball and Goodson, 1985). These exchanges resulted in teachers' experiences being situated more extensively within the wider political, social and economic contexts which influence their experiences of work and of career.

During this forty-year period, gender came to prominence as a critical variable in research on teachers and teaching. Some of the early studies of the teaching role made reference to the different role attributes of men and women in teaching (Floud and Scott, 1961) and Kelsall's statistical analysis (1963) focused on the characteristics of women teachers. Gender had always been a significant issue in research on the history of teaching (Tropp, 1957; Glenday and Price, 1974; Partington, 1976; Widdowson, 1980; Hoffman, 1981; Oram, 1983, 1985, 1987), but during the 1970s (Byrne, 1978; Deem, 1978) and increasingly in the 1980s, it was made a critical issue in education and some researchers focused their analyses on women teachers and women teachers' careers (Acker, 1983, 1987, 1988, 1989; Kaufman, 1984; Spencer, 1986; Shakeshaft, 1987; DeLyon and Migniuolo, 1989; Evetts, 1990).

THE RESEARCH ON HEADTEACHERS

Research on headteachers has undergone similar changes. Earlier studies (Allen, 1968; Barry and Tye, 1972; Houghton *et al.*, 1975; Lyons, 1976; Peters, 1976) focused on the role of the head, together with prescriptions for effective management. Prescriptions and recommendations for improving procedures in headteacher selection and for effective management have continued to be important in the research tradition (Morgan *et al.*, 1983; Earley and Weindling, 1987; Fullan, 1992). Case studies of Risinghill School (Berg, 1968), Summerhill School (MacKenzie, 1977) and William Tyndale School (Auld, 1976; Gretton and Jackson, 1976) and Sharp and Green's analysis (1975) of progressive primary education have illustrated some of the constraints within which headteachers operate and which limit their powers. Burgess (1986) has summarized these as heads' relations with local education authorities, governors, unions, parents, pupils, teaching and non-teaching staff. The interactionist perspective, meanwhile, has been concerned to emphasize the influence of headteachers in the day-to-day workings of schools (Ball, 1981; Burgess, 1983, 1984). The details of their everyday work was described by Hall *et al.* (1986). Gillborn (1989) considered heads' understanding of notions of 'high performance' and the difficulties they face in the current period of rapid educational change. A focus on the micro-politics of schools has resulted in headteacher leadership styles being analysed as aspects of their political activity and power in school organizations (Ball, 1987).

It is interesting to note that gender has not figured prominently in discussions of headship apart from discussions of gender differences in the numbers and distribution of headship posts. Thus nearly all teachers and headteachers of nursery and separate infant schools are women. The majority of primary teachers (81 per cent in 1990) are women, yet 51 per cent of primary headteachers are men (DES, 1990). In secondary schools 52 per cent of teachers and 80 per cent of headteachers are men. In general, women are marginalized less through numerical under-representation than through ghettoization and concentration in women's enclaves such as class teaching and, particularly, teaching in nursery and infant schools. In teaching, as in all careers, women are under-represented in senior management positions. This issue is beginning to receive research attention (Ozga, 1992).

Research and Gender Differences in Headship

Some women do achieve promotion to headship posts in schools, however. When researchers have focused their attention on gender differences in headship, the findings have been complex and sometimes contradictory. No significant gender differences have been found in terms of the definition of objectives, perceptions of the organization or task completion in school management. However, in terms of manner of execution of tasks and style of leadership, gender has been shown to be a differentiating variable. Most of the research on gender differences in leadership styles has been American, fairly small-scale and relatively inconclusive. Cochran (1980) noted that women principals were more effective at resolving conflicts, at motivating teachers and at acting as representatives rather than directors of a group. Adkison (1981) suggested that female compared with male principals were more likely to involve themselves in instructional supervision, to exhibit a democratic leadership style and to concern themselves with students. Such differences were confirmed by Shakeshaft's analysis (1987) of the woman principal as educational leader and master teacher compared with the principal as manager and administrator.

In Britain there have been several attempts to describe the leadership styles of headteachers (Lyons, 1974; Peters, 1976; Earley and Weindling, 1987) but few have confirmed gender differences. Indeed, significant gender differences have usually been denied (Earley and Weindling, 1987; Hall, Mackay and Morgan, 1986). Similarly, Ball's ideal types of leadership (1987) contained no reference to gender differences despite a thorough examination of women's careers in teaching and an analysis of the politics of gender. What happens, then, to the minority of women who do achieve promotion in the career to the management position of secondary headship? Is gender a significant factor in differentiating careers in teaching and experiences of headship? This study will include some exploration of these questions.

Chapter 1

Career History Study

THE CONTEXT AND OBJECTIVES OF THE PRESENT STUDY

Against this background of change in research focus and of renewed interest in interactionist theoretical perspectives and methodologies, I began a study of headteachers' careers. In 1985 I conducted a series of career history interviews with twenty-five women who were headteachers of primary and infant schools (Evetts, 1990). Then in the summer of 1990 I conducted career history interviews with twenty headteachers, ten men and ten women, of secondary comprehensive schools in two Midland educational authorities in England. At the time of the interviews the headteachers were struggling to cope with the first stages of local financial management (budgetary devolution) in their schools. They were also developing relations with their newly empowered governing bodies as well as managing the implementation of National Curriculum requirements and Standard Assessment Tests. These aspects of educational change were prominent in their perceptions of headteaching as work. In the autumn of 1992 these headteachers were contacted again in a questionnaire follow-up study of their experiences of educational change (Chapter 9). Throughout the study the objective was to try to understand what career meant to these promotion-successful individuals and they were encouraged to explain their own experiences of career and of secondary headship. My approach was thematic (Glaser and Strauss, 1967), i.e. allowing themes to emerge from the headteachers' accounts of their experiences.

The group of twenty headteachers was unusual only in that half of them were women. This sample of ten women represented 66 per cent of women heads of comprehensive schools in the two authorities, whereas the ten men heads represented a sample size of about 8 per cent. This over-representation of women was deliberate since the exploration of gender differences in career and in experiences of headship was one of the objectives of the research. In other respects the career history heads could be regarded as representative in that their schools varied in size from unit total group 8 to group 12 and their lengths of time in post varied from one year to twenty. The characteristics of the twenty heads reflected the general features of the headteacher profession and indeed the changes in the profession over time. Thus, for example, most of the men had achieved their headships when they were in their thirties or early forties; most of the women had achieved their first headship posts when they were in their forties or early fifties. The long-in-post headteachers, both men and women, had been promoted via the curricular route as heads of subject departments. For the newer headteachers, however, pastoral had been as important as curricular experience and indeed *both* had been required for the most recently appointed.

The career history sample was drawn up to reflect different sizes and locations of school (rural, suburban, inner city, etc.). The sample of women headteachers was selected first, with the men heads being selected afterwards to match, in terms of school size (unit total) and catchment area.

In the chapters which follow, extracts from the career history accounts are used to illustrate the themes of headship being examined. This was not quantitative research, however, and generalization to the population of headteachers is not undertaken. The objective of the research and the analysis of the career history data was rather to understand the differences in the experiences of career and of headship. Pseudonyms have been used throughout for the headteachers' names and sometimes for the names of places.

THEORETICAL PERSPECTIVES

The Concept of Subjective Career

The career history study was guided by interactionist principles: the interactionist concern with meaning, experience and the social construction of reality had resulted in the concept of 'the subjective career' (Woods, 1983). The distinction between objective and subjective dimensions of career was suggested by Hughes (1937), who contrasted the formal structure of posts, statuses and positions of the 'career ladder' (objective dimension) with individuals' own changing perspectives towards their careers — how they actually experience having a career (subjective dimension). Hughes described the subjective career as 'the moving perspective in which the person sees his life as a whole and interprets the meaning of his various attributes, actions and the things which happen to him' (Hughes, 1958, p. 409). Sikes *et al.* (1985) and the contributors to Ball and Goodson (1985) applied the concept in studying the careers of (predominantly) secondary teachers.

In the analysis of subjective careers, there is no prior assumption of promotion and progress, nor do job changes have to be regular or systematic, which has particular relevance to the study of women's careers. Also, the subjective career need not be centred solely on developments in the work sphere. As Sikes *et al.* have explained (1985, p. 2): 'the adult career is usually the product of a dialectical relationship between self and circumstances. As the result of meeting new circumstances, certain interests may be reformulated, certain aspects of the self changed or crystallized, and, in consequence, new directions envisaged.' In the subjective career, 'career contingencies' (usually events in the personal or private sphere which affect career) can become a major part of 'having a career', if that is how the individual perceives them.

When researchers focus thus on individual experience, career and work itself are shown to be diverse, not necessarily confined to a smooth unilinear development involving promotion and increased responsibilities. Some teachers might define career commitment as good classroom teaching rather than occupational mobility and might perceive career success as achieving a balance between work and family life rather than the achievement of promotion. The researcher focusing on the subjective career asks questions about how individuals see the problems and the possibilities; how they cope with and negotiate constraints and make use of opportunities; what they would perceive as the influences, the key events, decisions, turning points, and so on. This is the perspective that informed my analysis of the career history material.

Life and Career Histories: Their Use as Research Tools

The interactionist theoretical perspective revived interest in certain, relatively neglected, *methods* of research, such as observation, participant observation, field, and qualitative research (Croll, 1986; Burgess, 1982, 1985a, 1985b, 1985c); oral history (Vansina, 1985), the use of autobiographical accounts (Burgess, 1984a) and personal documents, such as diaries and letters as sources of data (Plummer, 1983). Most relevant to the present study was the revival of interest in life-history data and biography. The work of Faraday and Plummer (1979), Goodson (1981, 1983, 1991) and Bertaux (1981) succeeded in re-establishing life history as an important source of data, and other researchers such as Burgess (1983) and Beynon (1985) showed how institutional history as well as life history affected the operation of a school and influenced the lives and careers of teachers.

The use of life or career history has been attended by certain difficulties and potential pitfalls. There is no set of tried and tested research techniques that can be taken up and adapted by any researcher (Sikes *et al.*, 1985, p. 14). The method has weaknesses as well as strengths (Bertaux, 1981; Faraday and Plummer, 1979; Goodson, 1981, 1983, 1991; Woods, 1985). Problems of validity and generalization have been considered (Denzin, 1970; Beynon, 1985; Smith *et al.*, 1985, Corradi, 1991), yet the life-history approach has been claimed (Beynon, 1985) to be particularly appropriate for the study of subjective careers. Beynon claimed that the method is capable of stopping the huge gaps in our understanding of career, professional and personal lives, and moreover that life history data has advantages at three levels: (a) subjective, (b) contextual and (c) evaluative:

(a) Such data can be of particular value in illuminating individuals' subjective reality because it emphasizes subjects' interpretations of their everyday experience as explanations of behaviour.

(b) Life history grounds the individual life in the context of lived experience as well as in the broader social and economic system.

(c) Life histories reassert the complexities of lived experience for individuals and are less likely to result in the simplifications and generalizations that can arise when focusing on mass phenomena.

Beynon further claimed that the life histories approach enabled researchers to explore and build up sensitizing hypotheses and concepts: 'Life history material can tell us much about the socio-historical, institutional and personal influences on a career. It can help [the researcher] locate teaching in a wider temporal and inter-personal framework, incorporating external events that have diverted career trajectories (e.g. chance domestic factors or changes in the national economy) and pinpoint crucial benchmarks and phases in a career' (1985, p. 177).

Another argument in favour of using career histories is given by Abrams (1982), who argued that the process of becoming and the process of social reproduction are one and the same, and that in contexts where the determining weight of external forces appear to be overwhelming, the methodological argument for small-scale, detailed, qualitative research becomes strongest. Thus research into individual careers enables analysis to be done with sufficient detail to disclose what Abrams called the processes of becoming. The detail attained and the complexity and variation of experience revealed, discourages reification and enables researchers to see social reality 'as process rather than order, structuring rather than structure, becoming not being' (Abrams, 1982, p. 267).

It was with arguments such as these in mind that I decided to use personal histories in my exploration of what it means to become a secondary headteacher. I did not use complete life histories, however, but focused on the adult lives of the headteachers, concentrating on their post-school experiences, at work and in their personal lives. Thus I refer to the interviews as *career* history data. The intention was to collect details of each head's work and personal history and map these out so that different aspects of the career were interrelated. By gathering information on twenty subjective careers, I hoped to be able to say something about subjective careers in general. The individual narratives did indeed contain recurrent themes and general issues, making it possible to identify similarities and essential differences in the heads' experiences of subjective career.

The research was not intended to produce statistical generalizations, however. Mitchell's (1983) observations on the epistemological basis of qualitative research (e.g. case study and situational analysis) could also be applied to my career history material. She argued that such research relies 'on the validity of the analysis rather than the representativeness of the events' (p. 190). Thus the experiences of the headteachers in the career history study may well be representative of headteachers in general. But no claims will be made about their typicality. Rather, the aim is to increase understanding of the processes of becoming a headteacher and the variability in the experiences of a headteacher career.

Strategy: The History of the Concept

Individuals, while developing their careers, have to manage cultural and institutional processes of promotion. In looking at the management of constraints and opportunities, sociologists have found the concept of 'strategy' useful. The increasing popularity of the concept in recent sociological research and literature has been explained by Crow (1989) as in part a reaction against a structuralism that generates inexorable laws and, more positively, 'as something which offers the opportunity to go beyond the classic structure/agency dichotomy' (1989, p. 1). The concept of strategy was first developed as an instrument of analysis in interactionist theoretical perspectives (Goffman, 1968, 1970). In the sociology of education, as in other areas, it has been used increasingly to analyse research in which actions are interpreted as forming part of a strategy. Thus Woods wrote of its use in interactionist studies of education: 'it is where individual intention and external constraint meet. Strategies are ways of achieving goals' (1983, p. 9).

The advantage of strategic analysis is that such an interpretation of action prevents researchers portraying actors as passive, and looking at social institutions and structures as though they ultimately determine all outcomes. Rather the approach does emphasize the active part played by participants in adapting, adjusting and managing constraints and opportunities. Thinking in terms of strategies enables researchers to stress how role-learning involves an active process rather than passive conformity (Turner, 1962). Strategies will vary particularly according to the nature and types of external constraints and whether these are physical (space and time, for example), financial (resources), or more importantly perhaps for sociologists, constraints related to power, authority and control. Individuals will generally develop strategies to maintain and develop their interests, managing the organizational processes and the cultural constraints that govern the situation and using their own resources creatively to cope with this and to negotiate over outcomes. Sociologists have studied the strategic patterns that evolve as individuals cope with and manage particular sets of constraints over time. For example, Taylor and Cohen (1972) have so described the techniques that prisoners employ in the business of psychological survival, which involves extreme and formidable external constraints. Scott (1964) has studied the use of strategies in adjusting to the new social role needed by people who become blind; Plummer (1975) has done the same in connection with homosexuality.

The concept of strategy has also been used in the study of working careers. In this case, strategies are the ways in which individuals have (sometimes creatively) coped with, negotiated and managed cultural expectations and organizational structures. In the analysis of women's career strategies, this has involved women's management of cultural role expectations, both personal and public, together with their negotiation of organizational career ladders and frameworks. The strategies of women in particular occupations have been examined using methods such as life and career histories, biographies and auto-biographies. I explored the strategies developed by women primary head-teachers in their management of personal responsibilities and careers in teaching (Evetts, 1990). Using biographical accounts, Glazer and Slater (1987) analysed the strategies developed by individual women in medicine, psychiatric social work, university lecturing and social work, in their management of a male-defined model of career and career success.

Crow's (1989) examination of the use of the concept of 'strategy' served to remind researchers, however, that some social actions are more usefully investigated in terms of strategies than others. Particularly relevant to the analysis of headteachers' career strategies are two questions. Can actions which are not long-term, rational, conscious and purposive usefully be conceived of as 'strategies'? And can the actions of individuals who, as individuals, are relatively powerless be interpreted as strategic without at the same time disguising and camouflaging the real sources of power?

In the case of strategies for careers, it is necessary to emphasize that many careers are unstrategic in the sense that they do not demonstrate long-term development or a conscious and rational plan of action. Careers research has indicated that for a few single-minded and career-dedicated individuals, their lives could possibly be perceived as the working out of an early-perceived, external purpose and career goal. For the large majority of individuals, however, men and women, though particularly the latter, careers represent the working out of much shorter-term decisions, the taking up of opportunities presented and the negotiation of perceived constraints. Their career decisions are thus not so much part of a strategy as a way of life, an internal development of identity which involves reacting and responding to external changes. For many individuals, but particularly for women, career actions would fit more appropriately into a category of traditional action since career decisions illustrate reference to the past, continuity and lack of calculation, rather than the instrumentality and rationality that are implied by the term strategy.

Crow also argued that use of the term strategy in considering the actions of individuals could result in the neglect and obscuring of differences in power and influence in arriving at a decision. He concentrated his discussion on the differential power resources within collectivities but the point applies equally to an analysis of the actions of individuals. The use of the term strategy implies power resources to affect outcomes. In the case of strategies for careers, an emphasis on the creativity of individuals in devising career strategies and negotiating and managing constraints must not be allowed to obscure some of the resource differences related to gender. Men often have both cultural and organizational advantages in developing career strategies.

In general, the intellectual gains from using the term strategy as a way of linking cultural and institutional factors in the case of careers, those of women and of men, are widely acknowledged. Its use enables researchers to explore the interrelationship between structure and action by recognizing both the presence of structural constraints and the active responses of social actors to these. Career actions are no longer seen as completely determined by social forces, there *are* constraints but responses to them vary.

Nonetheless it is prudent to acknowledge that there are potential difficulties attached to describing careers as strategies: the imputation of rational, calculative, long-term planning and of power resources to influence career outcomes, might be inappropriate in analyses of some careers. The derivation of the term strategy and its links with warfare and business management need to be remembered. It might be the case that strategy, like career, is a gendered concept.

In the career history study, strategies for career became a feature in the analysis. I was interested in how the headteachers had perceived the constraints, the problems (e.g. the dual demands of teaching work and career and of personal, family and other responsibilities). I was also concerned to discover the similarities and the differences in the strategies that had been devised by some headteachers to enable them to fulfil perceived personal and family responsibilities and to develop their careers in secondary teaching. How had the heads perceived the constraints? How had constraints changed over the course of the career? Were there opportunities as well as constraints? How had some headteachers negotiated and managed the constraints and made use of any opportunities to develop their careers in both work and family life? Examining the strategies by means of which the heads had achieved personal as well as career goals, or had coped with specific constraints, would enable me to emphasize career as a process, and a continually changing process as goals were redefined and specific constraints came and went. The analysis could focus on the process of becoming a secondary headteacher.

The heads were continually developing strategies and then redefining them as responsibilities and constraints were encountered, negotiated and managed. Such 'strategies' could not be understood to mean only clearly-perceived and early formulated life plans and career intentions. Some individuals may have seen their careers in such a way, but for others career and personal responsibilities were in continuous process of change, negotiation and compromise. Often strategies were devised through chance and coincidence, procrastination and serendipity rather than through deliberate planning.

FROM CAREER HISTORIES TO SOCIAL STRUCTURES

It was possible also to go beyond the headteachers' strategies. Each of the headteachers contributed a narrative, an interpretation, a self-conscious retrospective account of what they considered important factors and influences in their own careers. When all the narratives were read together, it was possible to detect similarities and essential differences in their experiences of subjective career. In addition, however, these heads had supplied *information*: they had told of how they had got their various teaching jobs and their promotions, and how their careers had developed. In addition they had explained about the culture of headteaching as work. For those headteachers who had been long in post, they described changes in their work over time, enabling information to be gained about dramatic changes in the role of headteacher and the work culture of headship.

The linking together of the experience of becoming and of personal identity as a worker or professional has been a common theme of interactionist literature (Becker *et al.*, 1961; Lacey, 1977; Atkinson, 1981; Burgess, 1983; Atkinson and Delamont, 1985). The relationship between personal experience and social structure has also been explored. Implicit in such analyses is a two-way causality whereby the personal influences the social as well as the social constraining the personal. A unity between individual and social structure has often been emphasized. Berger and Luckmann (1967, p. 196) argued that 'identity is formed by social processes' and 'once crystallized it is maintained, modified or even reshaped by social relations'. Strauss (1977, p. 764) stated that 'identities imply not merely personal histories but also social histories'.

The strongest account of the interrelationship between the personal and the social is that of Abrams (1982), who argued that the processes of personal development and social reproduction are the same. He used numerous examples in order to demonstrate that both in the case of 'normal' and 'deviant' personal histories, the historical–social link is basic to the construction. 'Identities are assembled through the meshing together of two types of historically organized time: the life history and the history of societies' (1982, p. 250). He argued that identity, like society, is and can only be constructed historically and that structure and identity generate each other.

This linking of the historical and the social was taken up by Scott (1986) in respect of gender. She argued that we need to historicize gender differences and to recognize how the binary opposition between men and women is different in different historical periods and places. She believed that research which discovered universal gender differences (e.g. Gilligan's on moral reasoning) tended to end up by being ahistorical, defining gender as a universal, self-reproducing binary opposition, fixed and always the same (1986, p. 1065). Scott would prefer a denial of the fixed and permanent quality of the binary opposition and instead a focus on variation and change. 'To pursue meaning, we need to deal with the individual subject as well as social organization and to articulate the nature of their interrelationships, for both are crucial to understanding how gender works, how change occurs' (1986, p. 1067).

In order to understand the interrelationship between personal career and social conditions, therefore, we need to situate the personal history within the social history, that is the characteristics and constraints, the contexts and conditions for careers in teaching. Abrams (1982, p. 262) has argued that 'far from exempting us from the study of social structure any attempt to grapple with the problem of the historical formation of identity forces us in just that direction'. The career history data from the headteachers in the present study had to be explained in terms of the mechanisms and processes in the teaching profession which operated to attach individuals to jobs, and jobs to individuals. Wider external conditions would also have affected their subjective careers. But such influences did not only operate in one direction. The career histories and personal identities of particular headteachers would affect how schools were run, how teaching and learning were operationalized and how change or stability in education was produced or reproduced.

The headteachers' subjective careers had to be situated in the wider contexts in which teaching careers are constructed. For any individual career-builder the career contexts appear as given; individuals accept that these contexts are the structural conditions governing career progress and they are required to negotiate and manoeuvre within them. On a different level of analysis, however, career contexts are being developed and changed by those in positions of power to influence such contexts. Also, and as important, are the ways in which actions influence structures. A theme of this book is the duality of structure and action, the interrelationship between career actions and the reproduction or change of career and promotion structures (see Chapter 2).

The foregoing considerations of sociological interpretation and analysis are a necessary preliminary to examining the experience of becoming and being a secondary headteacher in England in the context of organizational change.

In the chapters that follow, the career history headteachers' accounts of their experiences will be used to illustrate how some heads have seen their work, their careers and the changes that have occurred in the work culture of headship. Chapter 3 will consider the experiences of promotion in the early and middle years; Chapter 4 looks at the continuities and changes in the selection process for headteacher posts; Chapter 5 focuses on the coordination of personal and public aspects of working lives; Chapter 6 investigates the development of management structures in schools; Chapter 7 discusses gender and headship; and Chapter 8 examines the career concerns of some secondary headteachers. A final chapter considers the new headteacher and the consequences for the task of headteaching of local financial management in schools and the opting out of some schools in England from local education authority control. But first, further elaboration is required of the model of career that is used in this book. The following chapter will thus consider the career conditions that form the background to the headteachers' experiences, first outlining the theoretical principles which inform the career analysis.

Chapter 2

Career Structures and Career Action in Teaching

RESEARCH BACKGROUND

In the 1950s and 1960s research on careers was dominated by the notion of organizational career structures. Careers were perceived as being *determined* by structural factors and conditions within organizations and places of work. Such an emphasis on structure was criticized for giving an 'oversocialized conception of man' (Wrong, 1961), and a reification of structural aspects of the social world (Evetts, 1992). It was followed by a focus on career action, subjective career and career strategy. This perspective offered a view of career as the series of choices and the negotiation of constraints made by an individual in the course of his/her career history. In the 1970s and 1980s a focus on career action seemed to offer the necessary counterbalance to organizational analysis (Gunz, 1989), but was acknowledged to have its limitations in seeming to overestimate the power of individuals to exercise control and to influence events.

Evidently there was a need to integrate the explanations of career structures with those of career actions. Various approaches have been put forward (Collins, 1975; Giddens, 1984; Knorr-Cetina and Cicourel, 1981). The present research adopted a model that relates structure and action through an analysis of processes of change. Changes in career conditions, expectations and outcomes are perceived as mutually affected and affecting.

This chapter examines the *structural conditions* for career-building in teaching and then introduces aspects of *career action*, i.e. how individuals build careers and seek promotions in teaching. Finally, it examines how the process of change can serve to link structure and action in the analysis of careers leading to secondary headships.

STRUCTURAL CONDITIONS FOR CAREER-BUILDING IN TEACHING

The importance of structural factors at the macro level of analysis for careers in teaching is usually acknowledged (Ball and Goodson, 1985; Sikes *et al.*, 1985). Such factors are: first, *external conditions*, including political and economic contexts and demographic change in the school-age population, which entails expansion or contraction in numbers of schools, teachers and headships. Such factors play an important part in influencing the general mood of optimism or pessimism amongst teachers and headteachers. The relative salary position (i.e. status) of teachers and heads compared with other professions and occupations is a similarly influential part of the economic context. *Legislative changes* constitute a second important career condition. A third condition is the salary and promotion structure for teachers and headteachers, i.e. the framework of posts and positions through which teachers' careers progress. Changes in the salary and promotion ladders for teachers and heads are important in altering the routes and paths by means of which teachers develop, understand and interpret their careers. These three career conditions as they relate to the present study of secondary headships will now be considered in turn.

External Conditions

The 1960s was a time of political optimism and economic expansion. The post-war increase in the birthrate, maintained until the 1960s, meant that the school-age population was increasing; schools were growing and new schools opening, requiring new teaching and headship posts. The consequent mood of optimism meant that new ideas were welcomed and tried and teachers and headteachers had scope and resources for experimentation (Richards, 1987; Lawn and Grace, 1987). The shortage of teachers and the opening of new schools provided plenty of promotion opportunities for teachers aspiring to headships.

Most researchers are agreed that in the 1980s the picture was very different: headteachers and teachers faced a general contraction of the education system. Nationally, there was a reduction in economic prosperity, an increase in central control of the financing and conduct of education, and a fall in school rolls. At the local level, this meant the amalgamation or closure of smaller schools, a cut-back in promotion posts and a general reduction in teacher and headteacher mobility. Such conditions, together with a general discontent among teachers over pay claims and a new salary structure, made teaching and headship a very different kind of occupation (Lawn and Grace, 1987). Thus in the 1980s external conditions consisted of a contracting education service and teaching profession and reduced promotion opportunities for teachers and heads. Sikes *et al.* (1985, p. 5) have commented:

> However, the disjunctive that probably runs deepest at the
> moment is that arising from the economic crisis, falling rolls and
> government policy, which have promoted cuts in educational
> resources and blockages (and in some cases stoppages) and
> re-routings in teacher careers which contrast greatly with the
> comparative days of plenty in the 1960s ... Promotions were

comparatively plentiful, over half of those in the late 1960s and early 1970s resulting from the creation of new posts.

Ball and Goodson (1985, p. 2) have given a similar description of changing educational conditions:

> Any attempt to portray the contemporary situation of teachers' work and teachers' careers must inevitably begin by recognizing the changing context within which this is undertaken and careers constructed ... From the 1960s we have moved from a situation of teacher shortage and apparently infinite possibilities for the expansion of educational provision to, in the 1980s, a situation of teacher unemployment and contraction in provision, with one or two exceptions, across the system as a whole.

They go on to discuss changes in the conditions of teachers' work and the conception of a career in teaching since the 1960s and how the consequences of changed external conditions can be different for different groups of teachers. Partington (1976, p. ix) claimed that such differing circumstances were likely to affect the status and promotion prospects of women teachers:

> The acute shortage of women teachers over three decades has been a very powerful aid in improving their relative position in teaching, but in the 1970s the demographic and teacher supply situations have changed very dramatically. A falling birth rate and a larger number of qualified teachers available for appointment than ever before will have implications for all teachers, but women teachers and especially married women teachers may well find themselves more vulnerable than men.

There is general agreement, then, that the expansion or contraction of the teaching profession has dramatic effects on the careers of men and women teachers and of heads and is a critical context of the teaching and head teaching career.

Legislative Changes

Recent legislative changes, in respect of education provision, finance and administration, have dramatically affected the contexts in which headteachers and teachers work. Here again, the consequences for heads' and teachers' careers are highly significant. This section will focus on the effects of legislation for local financial management in schools, the option of grant-maintained status, and the new arrangements for governing bodies, these being the most obviously relevant to headteachers' work and careers. This is not to deny the important consequences for the work cultures of teaching and headship of other new features in schools, e.g. the introduction of a National Curriculum and Standard Assessment Tests.

Local Financial Management. The transition to local financial management (LMS) has been variable from one LEA to another. According to the 1988 Education Reform Act, the change to formula-funded budgets and delegated powers for the financial management of schools was to be completed by the start of the 1993/4 financial year. The legislation had permitted such an adjustment period during which time schools could be protected from big alterations in budgets by being funded partially on an historic basis. However, most LEAs had moved to formula-funded budgets by 1990 and several had also implemented delegated powers, at least to secondary comprehensive schools.

Such local variation in LEA transition and implementation arrangements cannot disguise the general impact of LMS on headteachers' work. Under LMS budget management in schools is delegated to the governors, who become responsible for the deployment of resources within the school's budget, for determining the number of staff, for appointing and dismissing staff, for agreeing a management plan with the head, and for monitoring the school's achievement of its stated objectives. Headteachers have the responsibility for advising governors on budget management duties, and more scope, therefore, for devising aims and goals and for matching resource allocation to their stated objectives. Under LMS heads are thus better strategically placed than before to take decisions, advise, recommend, manipulate, bargain and negotiate. In most schools this has meant an extension of the powers and authority of the head and a redefinition of what it means to be a headteacher. Headship has always involved some financial management in that heads have had to negotiate with LEA officials over provisioning. But this has been according to widely accepted formulae and criteria. Following LMS, heads and their governors are responsible for managing and controlling most of the school budget, their decisions subject only to financial constraints.

Grant-Maintained Status. The option for schools to elect for grant-maintained status and to leave local authority control, subject to a vote in favour of such a change by interested parents, was also contained in the 1988 Education Reform Act. Subsequent refinements (1993 Education Bill) have proposed a Funding Agency to gradually take over from LEAs as soon as 10 per cent of pupils in an area are attending opted-out schools. Under LMS, schools control over 80 per cent of their budgets, the rest being used by the local authority to finance support services. With grant-maintained status, schools control their total budgets and are intended to buy in for themselves those services which the LEA provides for its own schools.

An early advantage of grant-maintained status for schools was that, as pioneers, such schools received more generous funding than LEA schools. This enabled headteachers and governors to hire more teachers, extend buildings,

17

redecorate and boost morale. Grant-maintained status has increased the business-management aspects of headship, therefore, and has accentuated the devolution of power to individual schools. It can be perceived as an additional step, beyond LMS, in increasing the powers, legitimacy and authority of headteachers as managing directors of school enterprises. Headteachers in grant-maintained schools are freed completely from the bureaucratic controls and formula-managed aspects of LEAs. The consequences for the headteacher career and daily work culture of headship are profound. A decline in aspects of educational leadership and consequent increase in financial and business management responsibilities have already been observed in the educational media (Wilce, 1989; Haigh, 1992) as well as in academic accounts (Morgan *et al.*, 1983; Evetts, 1991).

Governing Bodies. The 1986 Education Act altered the composition of governing bodies and extended their powers. The number of elected parent and nominated co-opted governors was increased and the number of LEA nominated governors reduced (Deem and Wilkins, 1992). Governors were to establish a secular curriculum policy, free from political bias, for their school. They were to play a part in headteacher appointments and they were to prepare a written annual report for parents.

Under the provisions of the 1988 Education Reform Act, the powers of governing bodies were further increased. Governors are now required to manage a budget which will eventually cover about 80 per cent of the total resources available to a school (the total budget in a grant-maintained school). They have staffing and salary responsibilities, set strategic goals, approve the head and senior management's policies for achieving those goals and consider reports on a school's performance (Levacic, 1989). The role of governors in school management is more immediate and direct as they now have real resources to control and responsibilities for the selection, appointment (and dismissal) of staff (Coopers & Lybrand, 1989).

The consequences for headteaching as work and for the careers of headteachers are becoming clearer. Headteachers now have to negotiate all decisions which require finance with their governing bodies. In general this has worked to increase heads' power and authority, since most governing bodies acknowledge the expertise of the head. There is nonetheless increased opportunity for conflict, should governing bodies disagree with headteachers' objectives and suggested means for attaining them.

The consequences for headteachers' careers are more speculative. In the selection process, candidates for headteacher posts will now have to impress the lay members of governing bodies. The consequences of this for some headteacher candidates, particularly women and members of minority groups, might be to increase inequalities in the achievement of headteacher posts.

In summary, legislative changes in respect of education provision, finance and administration have affected careers in teaching as well as the day-to-day work responsibilities of headship. Careers in teaching are now more to do with developing managerial and administrative skills, and headteaching has less to do with educational leadership and more to do with finance, business management and the management of educational change. There have been consequences for headteacher careers as the criteria of appropriate qualities for headteacher posts also change (see Chapters 4 and 9).

Salary and Promotion Structure

Until 1987 salary and promotion in teaching were regulated nationally according to the Burnham Scale and modifications to it (Hilsum and Start, 1974). Burnham recognized four salary scales plus senior teacher, deputy and headteacher scales. In 1987 the government replaced these with a basic scale for all teachers, separate scales for deputies and heads and a system of incentive allowances to be paid to teachers undertaking extra responsibilities.

The significance of the promotion ladder for teachers' careers has been studied in the past in terms of career paths or career routes (Hilsum and Start, 1974; Lyons, 1981), which involved analysing the various ways in which (sometimes large) samples of teachers had changed their jobs or remained in one job, had received promotion or not, over the course of their working lives. Such analyses could illuminate the different ways in which teachers had achieved a promotion position, say to Head of Department, and indicate the proportions of teachers achieving promotion positions and the characteristics of the 'successful' candidates.

The model of career resulting from such research was deterministic or prescriptive, for the researchers assumed that all headteachers and teachers had *wanted* promotion and desired to achieve the highest position they were capable of and that they had plotted their 'career maps' rationally (Lyons, 1981). It was also assumed that all heads and teachers were single-minded in their career objectives and that, although they might be differently informed as to the correct routes and procedures and differently equipped with promotional qualities and achievements, nevertheless they would work consciously and purposefully towards the promotion goal.

However, such assumptions can be misleading, especially (although not exclusively) in the study of women's careers. It should not be assumed at the outset that all heads and senior teachers have *wanted* promotion to management posts (Bennet, 1985); neither should it be assumed that women teachers who break their teaching service in order to care for their own children and whose careers do not match up to an assumed model of continuous service and regular promotion progress therefore have 'imperfect' or 'interrupted' careers. It should not be assumed that careers are only concerned with developments in the paid work sphere. Evidence is increasing that men as well as women are concerned to improve the quality of their personal life-styles outside rather than within work (Robertson, 1985; Scase and Goffee, 1989). For women and for men, public and private worlds need to be incorporated into our understanding of what it means to 'have a career'.

Within the teaching profession the headteacher position has tended to represent a career peak in terms of promotion progress. In English schools the headteacher salary used to be determined according to the size of the school, that is the school's unit total and grouping. With LMS, decisions about headteacher salary have been shifted away from LEA control, and power has been given to governing bodies to determine appropriate salary levels. There are, and always have been, some opportunities for career movement for headteachers from headship of a smaller to a larger school. However, research projects have indicated a substantial career stability among headteachers once in post (Earley and Weindling, 1988). Also, movement between headteacher posts, even if it occurs, does not necessarily constitute career *progression* for heads. Some of the headteachers interviewed in the career history study expressed concern about lack of further career opportunities (see Chapter 8). There have always been some heads who have moved on into adviser and inspectorships, LEA and even DES administration, college principal and directorships, and into research. So far numbers have been small, however, and lack of a further promotion ladder for headteachers is likely to remain an issue of career concern for some headteachers.

CAREER ACTION

Analysis of structural influences on careers such as discussed above has resulted in a deterministic and one-way causal model of career, i.e. a view of careers as being *determined* by structural, macro-factors and not subject to any influences that can be ascribed to career actors themselves.

If analysis of the structural influences on careers has certain limitations, what has resulted from regarding careers as individual experiences? From the Hawthorne experiments (Roethlisberger and Dickson, 1939) and early studies of informal work cultures, the emphasis has been on how individual actors influence and develop their own social frameworks and social worlds in formal organizations and professions. In the study of working careers, research into the perspectives and understandings of career-builders themselves seemed to offer the necessary counterbalance. Hughes (1937) identified the subjective dimension of individuals' own changing perspectives towards their careers; how employees actually experienced 'having a career'. Stebbins (1970) presented the subjective career as the actor's interpretation of events, which demonstrated that more than one kind of performance could be regarded as career 'success'.

In respect of careers in teaching, the idea of subjective career opened up new opportunities for studying heads' and teachers' experiences and the meaning to headteachers themselves of 'having a career' (Ball and Goodson, 1985). This approach involved mapping out an individual's work history, asking about aims, ambitions and intentions, and enquiring about perceptions of what happened and why (Sikes *et al.*, 1985). This resulted in diverse perceptions of career and of work itself (see pp. 6–7).

The analysis of subjective careers in teaching that involved no prior assumption of promotion and progress and did not concentrate solely on developments in the paid work sphere offered the possibilities of studying women's as well as men's careers, and of opening up career structures to the influence of heads' and teachers' own objectives and intentions (Bennet, 1985). Sometimes the concept of strategy was used in the analysis of teaching careers (see pp. 9–11).

It is important to note, however, that the subjective careers which resulted from such analysis were essentially *individualistic*: the model implied that *individual* participants were constructing subjective careers, coping with external constraints of career structures and systems using strategies that were particularistic and essentially apolitical. In focusing on the actors' contribution researchers had overcome the problem of underestimating the importance of heads' and teachers' own initiatives. But this was achieved by emphasizing the subjective responses of individuals and neglecting to consider the collective effect. Groups of individuals can (sometimes) affect changes in career routes, timetables and maps, and hence influence promotion ladders. Through established political channels (trade unions, professional associations and political parties) and through informal alliances and groupings within school organizations, collective action can (sometimes) influence, affect and re-define promotion structures and systems in particular schools, but eventually more widely. Also neglected were processes of change and the effect of change (other than as chance happenstances in the careers of individual heads and teachers) on career structures.

The analysis of subjective careers did not provide a completely satisfying explanation, therefore. In particular, the analysis of change had gone largely unexplored in respect of careers in teaching.

LINKING STRUCTURES AND ACTIONS

A recognition of the need to bridge the gap between structure and action in social theory has long been recognized. During the 1970s and 1980s, one of the suggested integrations involved a reconstruction of macro theory based on micro foundations (Knorr-Cetina and Cicourel, 1981).

In the study of careers the need for integration of structure and action levels of analysis was urgent and the micro-sociological challenge offered interesting possibilities. Harré (1981) and Giddens (1981, 1984) tried to reconcile the claims of structuralists and interactionists in respect of career models. According to Harré, the importance of the unintended consequences of social action is that actions do come to constitute systems. Giddens developed his notion of the duality of structure to explain how structure does consist of the rules and resources of social systems; how actors draw on these rules and resources which 'structure' their actions; and how such rules and resources are reproduced through the very same actions. So structures and systems do have properties which confront individuals in such a way that individuals are presented with a series of limited choices. In respect of careers in teaching, the implications are clear. In so far as heads and teachers develop their careers in particular ways, using the rules and resources which schools have devised, the unintended (and intended) consequences of such actions are that career patterns emerge. Individual choices are thereby constrained. Heads and teachers can choose to seek promotion (and increase their chances) by following in the paths of others before them or not to seek promotion (thereby increasing the chances of others). But future action is limited in that the system confronts individuals as a selection environment. According to this view, career patterns in teaching can be changed if sufficient individuals choose a 'different' route. Groups of individuals can thereby exert an influence on the course of social events. But career contexts and conditions nevertheless influence (may even determine) 'which "mutations" occurring in micro-social practices will "take" and persist to create actual social change' (Knorr-Cetina, 1981, p. 27).

Such an interpretation acknowledges the interrelationship of structure and action in accounting for both stability and change. It remains to be demonstrated, however, how both career structures and career actions can themselves be influenced by external and internal changes. By focusing on such changes, it becomes easier to ascertain the interrelationships between, and the processes which affect, both career actions and career structures in teaching.

ANALYSING CHANGE IN CAREER ACTIONS AND STRUCTURES IN TEACHING

An emphasis on processes of change may provide a way forward in career analysis. It is through interaction, confirmation and reproduction that micro-events are transformed into macro-social structures. But it is through external and internally required change that modification in career expectations and actions can bring about changes in career structures. It is necessary to 'identify the processes which contribute to the creation of macro-structures by routine inferences, interpretations and summary procedures' (Cicourel, 1981, p. 51). It is also necessary to clarify how macro-structures affect, influence, constrain and confine micro-interactions and -interpretations. But it is important in addition to analyse how changes in contexts and circumstances, say in administrative arrangements and/or in demand for and supply of teachers and headteachers, can affect macro-structures as well as micro-interpretations.

In the analysis of career in teaching, it should be possible to use the structural and interactionist approaches outlined above to explain objectivization and subjectivization as the interlocking processes which inevitably they are, and to show how the objectivization of career routes results in particular subjective responses of teachers and heads, and how subjectivization results in the reproduction and sometimes the modification of objective career structures. Examining the processes of career in teaching and headship in the context of change enables an exploration of who is re-defining promotion ladders and why. In most cases this will involve the interactions and negotiations of macro actors, such as representatives of employers and governments, trade unions and professional associations. Other questions then follow, such as how the resultant compromises and agreements between macro actors are operationalized and encodified in new regulations and procedures by means of which individuals come to interpret, explain and account for their career experiences. In other words how changes become incorporated into new reality-defining structures and systems in the separate schools and in the experiences of individual heads and teachers. Likewise, in the analysis of change, the experiences of head-teachers and teachers are fundamental. When sufficient numbers of heads and teachers alter 'established' career patterns via their actions, then career structures and systems are modified and changed. Experiences of career are part of the same mutually reinforcing process whereby actions and structures interact and reinforce a career outcome. Situations of change are the best scenarios in which to observe and analyse such a process.

It is important to emphasize that change is a constant feature of experiences of career in teaching. The modification of administrative and managerial arrangements seems to be a regular occurrence in schools. Expansion and contraction of the teaching profession, and of supply and demand for teaching personnel, mean that schools are constantly adjusting their career and promotion ladders. Political decisions and ideologies continually affect both schools and the educational service. Legislative changes re-define career and promotion ladders. There is no shortage, then, of career changes for analysis in the attempt to understand the process of career. There are numerous important contemporary examples. For headteachers, political changes such as the possible demise of LEAs might mean dramatic alterations in the management of education, which could have important career implications for both current and aspiring headteacher post-holders. Within schools, jobs change to become careers (as with the devolution of finance and budget management) when promotion layers and levels are attached to secretarial and administration positions. Or changes in job specifications can make new career routes available as, for example, when changes in the organization of schools require different qualifications and experiences in candidates for career promotion.

We will begin the analysis of the career process, following Cicourel, by considering routine work-place interactions, the work cultures that develop in schools and out of which internal bureaucratic practices develop which are used to reach decisions about promotion potential (see Chapter 3). Then we need to analyse how decisions on the necessity for change in management and promotional structures are reached and are passed down through the selection processes to become operationalized in the school context (Chapter 4). We need also to consider the ways in which such practices and decisions are operationalized in terms of the career development of individuals (Chapter 6). How are practices changed such that new ladders and new movements between positions are identified or ladders are closed off and new job descriptions are implemented (Chapter 3)? If the process of change in career patterns is in the forefront of researchers' minds, then it becomes easier to avoid the problem of over-determinism by career structures. Likewise, if the process is seen as the operationalization of decisions reached by macro actors, then differentials in power resources to define and make use of career rewards will be a fundamental aspect of the explanatory model.

At the same time we need to consider what individual heads and teachers themselves know about the human capital characteristics required in promotion and selection procedures and how they learn about the possibilities of change; what they know about how decisions concerning promotion practices are made and are changed over time; how their career choices are affected and how their career decisions are arrived at (Chapters 3 and 4). By these means we might learn how career structures become real and at the same time how structures alter and are changed. In such ways the micro and macro processes in the school and elsewhere that can enable us to explore and perhaps even explain career are constantly interrelated and interacting.

In the case of teaching, which has a national career promotion structure, then, in addition to the school, it is necessary to consider local, regional and national interactions. These involve the procedures by means of which assessment characteristics and the contractual areas of responsibility of particular work roles and promotion procedures are negotiated and come to be changed and re-defined (Chapter 9). Such interactions and negotiations have been termed 'macro-actions' by Callon and Latour (1981), who argue that such macro-interactions need the same framework and the same methods of analysis as micro-situations. They only differ in terms of power relations and resources and in the extent of their networks. Thus when analysing macro-interactions the researcher is analysing the way macro-actors (say the representatives of teacher unions, employers and government) develop internal bureaucratic practices and procedures which are used to arrive at decisions about promotion requirements and develop new structures of managerial positions.

Career actions can alter structures just as structures affect strategies. The intentions of micro-actors and of macro-actors should be analysed in respect of the processes which contribute to the change of macro-career structures. Similarly the influence of macro-processes on the experiences and interpretations of career of individuals should be examined. We need to understand the complex processes which are cultural (gender, for example) and political (legislative changes and ideological beliefs) as well as functional and strategic (such as job specifications and changes in specifications for particular positions). These are the processes whereby career structures *become* real so that individual teachers and headteachers come to see their work, their lives and their careers in terms of such structures (Chapter 8). So careers are cognitive in that they are understood, experienced and used, but they are also normative in that they are constraining and limit choices of action. By analysing processes of change we can have such interrelations between structure and action constantly in mind. Thereby we might be able to prevent both the over-determinism of structure and the 'oversocialized conception of man' (Wrong, 1961) as well as avoiding the denial of the existence of reality-defining structures and systems of power (Gidden, 1984). We need to have constantly in mind the mutually reinforcing processes of career structures and career actions; of how structures arise out of interactions and how actions are influenced by structures.

These are the themes which provide the framework for the chapters in this book. The mutually reinforcing processes of career structure and career action in teaching and headship will be examined and interrelated. The career strategies of a group of headteachers interviewed about their career histories will be used to illustrate how promotion structures in teaching become institutionalized and reproduced. In addition, however, the focus will be on change; how career structures in teaching and headship have changed and are changed. Only by beginning to understand how change affects both career structures and career actions can we begin to devise strategies that will be appropriate for changing career structures.

Chapter 3

Promotion in the Career: The Early and Middle Years

In the existing research on teachers and teaching it has been the first phase of the career, teacher socialization, that has received most attention (Lacey, 1977; Sikes, 1985; Cole, 1985). In addition, particular crises in the teaching career, both institutional and personal, have also been considered (Riseborough, 1981, 1985; Measor, 1985; Beynon, 1985). In his analysis of the process of becoming a teacher, Lacey identified four phases of socialization for student-teachers (honeymoon period; search for materials; crisis; learning to get by). In considering more established teachers, Hammersley (1977) and Woods (1981) have refined Lacey's original model. In addition Burgess (1986) has argued that whenever teachers take up new posts and new responsibilities in post then they are again placed in the role of novices and have to re-learn their new tasks. In particular, teachers who achieve promotion, and throughout their careers take on additional managerial and administrative responsibilities, will have to learn anew the task and the norms, relationships and expectations governing it. In secondary schools teachers are appointed to positions in departmental structures and pastoral posts in year or house systems. Teachers then choose to undertake additional responsibilities such as organizing school trips and editing the school magazine. They are unlikely to receive an allowance for such activities but are able to show willing and to indicate that they are ready and able to take on extra responsibility. Most teachers' careers subsequently involve promotion into middle management positions such as heads of departments and heads of houses and years. In return for taking on such administrative responsibilities teachers are given allowances and promotions but also they gain status and seniority. In turn this influences the kinds of teaching they undertake since, as Lacey (1977) showed, heads of department receive both more non-teaching periods for their administrative duties, more sixth-form work and fewer bottom-stream pupils.

Some sociologists have argued that teaching is relatively career-less compared with other kinds of non-manual work. Purvis (1973) argued that structural variables such as the flat career structure, the scale of remuneration and the authority structure in schools meant that most teachers had few promotion opportunities. Lortie (1975) and Dreeben (1970) have described teaching in the USA as career-less. However, Sikes et al. (1985) have argued that the great majority of teachers in England, both men and women, do expect some kind of promotion. The career structure in teaching is a flattened pyramid, but it is a hierarchical structure which involves specialisms, divisions of duties, responsibilities and powers, and hierarchical levels of command. Others have argued that hierarchical management is a growing feature, particularly in secondary schools, as teachers are becoming proletarianized (Ginsburg, *et al.*, 1980; Lawn and Ozga, 1981) as a result of the trend towards greater centralization of control of the curriculum and growing demands for teacher accountability. Thus the moves towards a centralized curriculum (National Curriculum), new forms of assessment (Standard Assessment Tests) and demands for teacher appraisal, all indicate a greater centralization, an advance in bureaucratization and an increase in hierarchical structures of management which run counter to professionalism and more collegial forms of management.

Career maps (Lyons, 1981) of teachers' careers in schools are hierarchical, therefore. Career prospects depend on seeking and making the most of career opportunities and on recognizing and adjusting to organizational structures in particular schools (Burgess, 1983). But it is important to emphasize that career structures are not stable or static. They are constantly changing both within particular schools and as schools in general adjust to new educational (and political) philosophies. Thus Lacey (1970) demonstrated how internal reorganization at Hightown Grammar School resulted in a new house system which meant teachers had to decide whether career opportunities were better in the departmental or house system. Similarly Burgess (1983) demonstrated how in Bishop McGregor School the house heads had more power and status than departmental heads and how it was from among house heads that teachers were recruited to be deputies (Burgess, 1986). It is equally important, however, to recognize the significance of more general educational changes for teachers' careers and career prospects. The change to comprehensive schooling, which was a long tortuous process in England, had a profound effect on teachers' careers. Riseborough (1981) examined how former secondary modern school teachers were displaced by subject-centred staff in the change to comprehensive schooling. Using teachers' own accounts he demonstrated how such teachers lost all career prospects with the result that they opposed the head and everything he was trying to introduce.

For the headteachers in the career history study, when they were young and aspiring teachers, the change to comprehensive schooling was just the opposite. This change presented them with an opportunity to develop their careers and, for some, to receive very rapid early promotion. The interrelationship of career action and career structure will be demonstrated by considering first the effect of changing external conditions and how some of the career history heads were able to make the most of comprehensivization. Then any gender differences among the career history heads will be examined. Were the men and women in the career history group differently equipped to make career and promotion capital out of the change to comprehensive schooling?

CHANGING CAREER CONDITIONS: COMPREHENSIVE SCHOOLING

The change to a system of comprehensive secondary schooling from what was predominantly a selective system, whereby pupils were sorted into 'appropriate' schools according to performance in an 11+ examination, took a long time in England. Until the 1980s, the administration of English schools had been described as a partnership between central and local government where, in respect of both policy and the financing of schools, a degree of autonomy was allotted to local education authorities in the implementation of central government recommendations. The first comprehensive secondary schools were established following the Butler Education Act of 1944 in local authorities such as Leicestershire which did not establish selective secondary schools. In the 1960s, and particularly in the 1970s, the large majority of LEAs eventually changed their school systems, moving from academically selective to comprehensive catchment arrangements. However, a minority of schools in particular LEAs (e.g. Buckinghamshire and Warwickshire), continued to operate selection procedures to determine school intakes. In the 1990s there is a possibility of some schools returning to selection as a number of schools opt out of LEA administration and elect to become grant-maintained.

Secondary school reorganization affected schools in different ways. Some schools were closed but most were either amalgamated or converted to become comprehensive schools. The effects on teachers' careers were also variable. Riseborough (1981) showed how a group of former secondary modern school teachers lost status and any hopes of career promotion when their school was amalgamated with a grammar school. These teachers felt that their particular teaching skills, acquired in the secondary modern school context, had been devalued and young teachers with different educational ideals were appointed and promoted over them. This particular reorganization caused career problems for some of this group although, as Sikes *et al.* (1985) noted, for others it opened up new career prospects particularly on the pastoral side.

Another group who experienced difficulties as a result of school reorganizations were some ex-grammar school teachers. As Sikes *et al.* (1985, p. 9) have commented these were teachers who came into teaching through their interest in the academic pursuit of a subject. Then, following reorganization, they were not only required to teach more subjects and to undertake pastoral responsibilities but also were required to teach groups of mixed ability. They found themselves being asked to do a different kind of job to the one they had come to expect and were required to undergo an identity change in order to cope. Again, however, it must be emphasized that for teachers in this group who were able to take on the new ideology and the diversified responsibilities, expanded career opportunities were also available.

Sikes *et al.* concluded that in general it was the group of mid-career teachers who were most likely to be adversely affected in career, promotion and identity terms. This was because these were teachers who were likely to have been well settled in their previous jobs and who were required to make a profound change. They had little alternative since they were not qualified to do anything else. Older teachers had the option of retirement or of time-serving careers. Younger teachers were perhaps best placed to benefit since their college training had prepared them for the comprehensive ideology. They had an appropriate mix of academic and pastoral experience and they were well placed to handle the organizational changes and to benefit themselves in career and promotion terms.

Both men and women headteachers in the career history group had been able to benefit from comprehensive reorganization. They had made the most of such changes in their early and mid-careers. Early in his career Mr Draper had been promoted via the head of subject route. Then, at age 37, he made a conscious career decision to seek wider pastoral experience.

After three years, I moved to (a) grammar school which is in the city, as Head of Chemistry. I became Head of House and a sixth form tutor as well as Head of Science and I think at the time I went from B to a C and eventually to a D, Head of Department. I think the department had a considerable number of successes, certainly we sent somebody to Oxford every year that I was there. In my Diploma in Education I studied the integration of pupils from bi-lateral schools into the sixth form of a grammar school. And by 1967 there were more pupils coming from bi-lateral schools into the sixth form than there were actually coming from the school's own fifth year. It was very interesting as a sixth form tutor to find out the difficulties of integrating pupils into the sixth form. Very interesting.

I had a good position in that school and I could have stayed for ever but I did see comprehensive education coming. A friend and myself talked it over and tried to anticipate what might happen. In the end I decided that, since comprehensive education was coming, then it would be a good idea if I found out how the other half lived. So, therefore, *for that reason* rather than promotion, I applied for and got the deputy headship in 1968 of (a) bi-lateral school.

And as deputy head I lost a stone and a half the first term I was there and finished up in hospital in 1968 with an irritated gall bladder. That was the effect that changing from a grammar school with a well-run department and everything, to a bi-lateral or secondary modern school had on me. I am now glad I made that choice because at least I was young enough to absorb the shock. One of the things that saddened me was that a lot of my friends, when comprehensive education came in, were at an age when they could not take the shock and a lot of good colleagues disappeared, mental breakdowns and so on.

(Mr Draper)

For other heads in the career history group, the change to comprehensive schooling was all-important in their early career promotions. Some were promoted following grammar school teaching experience (Mr Johnson). Others were promoted after secondary modern school experience (Mr Bennett and Mr Stevens).

I was beginning to feel that the constraints of the formal, the more formal grammar school system were not going to satisfy me for the rest of my career. And comprehensivisation was really getting into its stride in the early and mid-1960s, and at that point I began to apply for Head of English faculty posts, really throughout the country. And it was at that stage of education when there was a lot of expansion going on and the opportunities for promotion were tremendous. And I went for interview to [_____] which was then in Cheshire and was appointed to Head of English there. And that was a fortuitous move in the sense that the school, when I joined it, was reorganizing from a fairly successful grammar school to a comprehensive school and so I was right in at the beginning. In a situation where the headteacher had just been appointed, I took over a tricky department in that the former Head of English stayed on in the school as a senior teacher, although I am not sure that was his title then, and also within the department was one of the deputy heads. And she was charming, but very traditional. And between them I had some fairly formidable opponents with the new methods that the head wanted me to bring into the school.

(Mr Johnson)

I then moved to Harlow New Town, to do the same job in a comprehensive and that was the start of the period of time when the nation was changing towards comprehensive schools. The one decision then was with three years secondary modern experience whether to move into a grammar school, or to move into a comprehensive school and luckily, as it's gone, I took the right decision, which was to move into a comprehensive school. . . .

I became a House Master and was in charge of careers at the school and then a Head of Year. They were almost accidental appointments, there were no immediate promotions; it was 'would you take on', which I did, being keen and willing in those days. . . .

We were still in rented accommodation in Harlow but at that stage the housing authority put the kind of house we were in on the open market to buy at some ridiculous price of about £4,000. I think my salary was a £1,000 a year and there was no way, no way even then, I could afford to buy a house, I mean the mortgage was too much. So I started looking for promotion. There was a brand new school opening up in Yorkshire and I applied, among a number of applications, for a Head of Year post at Grade E, being truly optimistic, and much to my surprise I got the post. So in August 1968, we moved as a family up to [_____] and I moved in effect from a scale 2 to a grade E at the age of 31, which was very rapid, a very significant promotion, from almost bottom of the scale to the top in one move. I've always put that down to the particular circumstances of the time which saw a marked shortage of teachers who had experience in comprehensive schools, at the time when comprehensive schools were really coming on-stream. So clearly a new comprehensive school was looking for teachers with at least some comprehensive experience. There weren't a lot of us about and I think that gave me the edge which allowed such rapid promotion and I think those days have gone.

(Mr Bennett)

I started off teaching History. When the school became comprehensive with a new head, we then moved to Integrated Humanities. I was very keen on that and I got involved and I became the coordinator for that. That was unpaid, I mean those were the days where you worked in a job for two years and the head then said to you 'Oh you did that pretty well, I'll now give you an allowance', you know, the sort of thing these days that you can't get away with at all. So I did that and then I became Head of Humanities after some time but it was mainly responsibility for lower school integrating.

(Mr Stevens)

For the women headteachers also the change to comprehensive schooling had provided similar career opportunities for those willing to endorse the new ideology and more extensive pastoral responsibilities. Promotion via a subject route (Miss Reeves) and via a mixture of pastoral and academic responsibilities (Mrs Morley) was linked in with comprehensive changes.

I was reasonably successful as Head of Department in a grammar school, which was a lovely job. We had, my colleagues and myself, we had a lot of success with getting people on to reading History at university and that sort of thing which was all very pleasant and very easy to do....

I was then in my early thirties and I thought it looks as if I'm not going to get married after all....

So I thought I'd better take this a bit seriously. So I started to go to courses and things like that. And the world was going comprehensive. We're looking at the period of 1965 and I thought well if I'm not really careful I shall miss the boat here. Philosophically I was somewhat predisposed towards the idea of comprehensivisation, having had really no experience of it. I had done my teaching practice at a comprehensive school but that was in the remote past by then....

So I then applied, never having taught in a comprehensive school at all except on teaching practice, for the deputy headship of a comprehensive school in Norwich, which to my enormous surprise I got. The opposition wasn't very promising, so perhaps I was best of a poor field, I don't know. And that was a culture shock, yes! I can't pretend that I liked it, I didn't.

(Miss Reeves)

In 1974 Pennington went comprehensive and career-wise it put me in the right place at the right time. By then I had got to grips with the A level and I had proved that I could get good results in the subject, which to the head at that time meant I was a good teacher. She very much judged results and how you taught as going together. I had experience by then of secondary modern, junior, further education, bi-lateral, whereas most of the teachers at that school had experience of just grammar school. So I was given the job of welcoming in the first comprehensive year as Head of First Year which then became Head of Lower School when there were two years. Subsequently the Houghton agreement meant that we could have a second deputy and there was a deputy head pastoral job advertised which I applied for and I got. So within a few years I wasn't what I set out to be, which was Head of Religious Studies, I was deputy head of a comprehensive school.

(Mrs Morley)

Headteachers in the career history group had been able to make use of changing external conditions in order to further their own careers. The traditional route to a headship post was widely acknowledged to be via head of a subject department and from there to a deputy headteacher position. The change to comprehensive schooling widened and extended the recruitment criteria: some pastoral experience together with support for comprehensive educational ideals and comprehensive experience was desirable in candidates for promotion in the 1960s and 1970s. Some of the career history teachers had followed the subject route to headship but others were forming a new career structure, based more on pastoral responsibilities as head of year or head of house or administrative duties to integrate formerly separate subject areas. The strategies of the headteachers in their early and middle careers were perceived by them in retrospect to have been to support the educational changes and to equip themselves with the necessary wider experiences. At the same time such strategies were working to modify and extend the career structures within teaching. Pastoral as well as academic expertise, and later administrative and managerial experience, were now required for promotion in teaching.

GENDER DIFFERENCES IN EARLY AND MID CAREER

Teachers do not all follow the same occupational career path, nor is the life career similar in other respects. All teachers have their personal biographies. For the headteachers in the career history group, however, there were some common features in their career developments in addition to the considerable differences in their individual experiences. Some of the similarities in their accounts can be summarized as gender differences in career. The women's experiences, like the men's, had varied but there were some common features.

Among the career history headteachers there were no gender differences in the original decision to become a teacher. A few, both men and women, had been strongly committed to a career in teaching:

> Well I went to university to be a teacher; I had always wanted to be a teacher. I did as a child consider archaeology which was an interest but never really seriously considered anything other than teaching.
>
> (Mrs Ince)

> I always wanted to teach. I saw it as a good career.
>
> (Mr Oakes)

For most of the career history heads, however, they had drifted into teaching rather than making a positive career choice.

> I applied to go on a Colonial Services Course but my mother was very unhappy at the thought of me disappearing off into Africa so I did a career switch. I did the PGCE course largely because I couldn't think what else to do at that juncture. I'd thought, right I'll do that and teach for a couple of years and see what else turns up.
>
> (Mr Clifford)

33

I was one of those people who did not make a positive decision that teaching was the career that I wanted. But I was lucky, fortunate, in that when I did begin to teach I realized how much I enjoyed it.

(Mr Johnson)

I was working in the Civil Service when my younger sister was finishing her sixth form education. She brought college prospectuses home and I started to look at them. I thought well if she can go to college so can I. Then the first time I got in front of a class I realized I loved it.

(Mrs Dexter)

I hadn't the least intention of going into teaching when I finished my degree. I looked around for a variety of occupations and I wasn't too fussy what I did. I took a job as a shipping clerk but it was going to lead nowhere. My friends had all gone into teaching and they said well it's not too bad so I thought it'll do for a year or two till I get married and I drifted into teaching.

(Miss Reeves)

Both men and women heads in the career history group explained their decisions to teach as non-decisions, as drifting. For the women heads, however, there was an attraction: teaching was *convenient* as an occupation for women.

The last thing I was going to be was a teacher. I was going to do research but I flunked out of that because I was pregnant and we got married at Christmas. I took up some part-time teaching, introducing French experimentally into primary schools. It was just a little job, you know, but it went on from there.

(Mrs Cooper)

I had planned to go to America for a year but in the meantime I got engaged and it didn't fit our future domestic plans. So I gave all that up and came home without a job and needing to work for a year to get some money to get married. I got a job teaching English but I also taught some History and some Maths. Poor kids!

(Mrs Selby)

For the women heads teaching was an appropriate occupation, it was convenient for women. In taking up teaching as an occupation, either by embarking on training or by taking up part-time or supply-teaching posts, these women were not transgressing traditional gender expectations. Teaching as an occupation could be fitted in with other gender responsibilities to home and to family.

Teaching as an occupation involved no gender conflicts. However, teaching *as a career* did entail other sorts of expectations, namely that the teacher would seek promotion by taking on administrative responsibilities and subsequently managerial positions within schools.

In respect of job changes and early career promotions there were gender differences in the experiences of the men and women headteachers in the career history group. In general the women were slower to start promotion developments in the career. In contrast the men headteachers in the career history group had assumed responsibilities early in their careers and had achieved significant promotions while in their twenties and thirties.

> After a couple of years, the Head of Lower School decided to retire and I applied for and got that post because it offered more scope than the one I already had. I had been in charge of Geography and external examinations. I'd introduced A level and CSE into the school.
>
> The head could see that re-organization of the school was imminent and he'd decided to move on. The two deputies had made it quite clear they wanted nothing to do with reorganization because they were both in their late fifties and looking forward to retirement. So the head encouraged me to involve myself in the school timetable and curriculum development. Initially he did the paperwork and I put the timetable together. Then he let me do the paperwork under his guidance. Then in the third year he let me do the lot.
>
> (Mr Hall, first headship at age 37)

> The first job was in a boys' grammar school as an assistant teacher in the English Department; stayed there three years. Moved to second in department in an English Department in Blackpool. Grammar school for boys as it then was; stayed there three years. Moved to Bury in Lancashire as Head of English Department in a secondary modern school, stayed there three years. Moved as Head of Department in a comprehensive school in Stockport, Manchester; stayed three years. Was promoted to senior teacher and then moved to deputy head at a comprehensive school in Rochdale, Manchester; stayed there three years. Moved to a headship in Skelmsdale New Town, comprehensive school; stayed five years.
>
> (Mr Lane, first headship at age 36)

> Well, there was a shortage of chemistry teachers and I went as Head of Department in my first job, to an independent school ∪nd I acted there as Head of Science and Housemaster and

> stayed there for four years, four nice years. That then enabled
> me to go as Head of Chemistry to a technical school in Sheffield.
> I stayed there as Head of Chemistry for six years. The school
> grew and my graded allowance grew with it. Then I went as
> Deputy Head to another technical school in Gateshead and
> stayed there for six years.
>
> > (Mr Wells, first headship aged 40 but with two years
> > National Service)

By taking on administrative and managerial responsibilities early in their careers the men headteachers in the career history group had achieved significant promotions while they were still young. Thereafter their promotions had been regular and steady. For the women headteachers, however, their promotions had proceeded more slowly. This was the case whether the woman had remained single and childfree (Miss Hollis) as well as with women who had married and had children of their own.

> I was 32 when I got a post as Head of Religious Education. At 34
> I got a deputy headship. But I was 45 before I got a headship post.
>
> > (Miss Hollis)

Mrs Ince had had eight years out of teaching bringing up her own family. When she returned to teaching, job moves were necessitated by her husband's developing career in teaching rather than her own career. She was able, however, to achieve promotions as well as widening her own experience.

> Then my husband got a headship so we moved and I looked for
> another job. I became Head of English in a middle school partly
> because I thought that my husband would be very occupied
> being a headteacher. Our children were still quite young at the
> time and I thought that job would not be as demanding and
> time-consuming as A levels. So I thought that might be
> easier. . . .
> In the first year there I applied for and got another job as
> Head of English at a grammar school. I stayed there five years
> and was very happy. Then my husband got a headship of a
> larger school. So we moved to Sheffield and I was looking for
> jobs. There were no jobs for Head of English, the only jobs that
> came up were for deputy heads. I applied for three jobs and got
> the second.
>
> > (Mrs Ince, first headship at age 47)

Mrs Morley's career in teaching had been long and very varied. She had four breaks for childcare and did extensive periods of part-time teaching in order to fit in with childcare responsibilities. Her wide experience of teaching in different kinds of schools is recounted earlier (see p. 32) and she achieved her first headship post at age 53.

The career of Mrs Peters was similar in that her promotions had started later and proceeded much more slowly. Breaks for childcare and moves determined by her husband's career had likewise provided Mrs Peters with very wide experience of teaching in different kinds of schools.

> When my child was two we went to Uganda for two years. I did a term teaching in a secondary school there which was all black or Asian children, teaching English. I did that for a term and then I moved to the technical college where I taught English to adult students and liberal studies.
>
> Then when we came back to England I did a term's training for teaching emotionally disturbed children in Sheffield. That led to a job in a special school. After that I went back into mainstream secondary, teaching the lower ability end, English, Special Needs and so on. I did that for two years. Then I moved to another larger secondary school in Sheffield to the first scale post I'd had. That was in 1973 and I taught Special Needs, English, Maths and Humanities. I did that for three years and then my husband got a job in [_____] so in 1976 we moved and I got a job on a scale 2 which was for lower ability English and Special Needs. I was there until 1985 and I moved from that post to a scale 3, Head of Year. I did that for about a year and a half. Then I was offered a Head of Faculty job on a D, a scale 4, a Head of Guidance Faculty, still teaching Special Needs. I did that for three years then I got a deputy headship which was a pastoral job. I stayed there for three and a half years.
>
> (Mrs Peters, first headship at age 45)

Mrs Selby's career had also started slowly and there had been frequent job changes for her husband's career. Like most of the women heads, Mrs Selby's experience in teaching had been wide and very extensive.

> Before my son was born I had moved from unfinished probationer via primary schools to second in an English Department.
>
> When my son was about two and a half I started again and did supply work, part-time, and teaching basically English. I moved schools a couple of times and gradually increased my hours. After about five years at [_____] school I eventually became Head of Religious Education and then after the appointment of a new head, I got a Head of House post.
>
> (Mrs Selby; first headship age 43)

In general, then, amongst the headteachers in the career history group there were some gender differences in the early and mid-career experiences of promotion. There were no gender differences in the initial decisions to become a teacher. For both men and women heads, a few had seen teaching as a vocation and as something they had always wanted to do. Most of the heads, both men and women, had drifted into teaching, however. Their intentions had been to give teaching a try and then they had discovered that they enjoyed the work and were successful in the classroom. For the women in the group, however, teaching was perceived as a convenient occupation in that it enabled some resolution of gender dilemmas. Teaching, more than other occupations, enabled women to combine paid and unpaid work responsibilities.

Once engaged in teaching in schools, the careers of the men and women had taken different forms. For the men headteachers, they had assumed responsibilities early and career promotions had followed either regularly and systematically or alternatively in large jumps. The older male heads had been promoted through the head of subject route while the younger heads had more often combined head of subject and pastoral responsibilities. For the women headteachers who were unmarried, they also had assumed responsibilities and gained promotions early in their careers, although the promotion to headteacher had taken much longer. For the married women heads, their promotions had started later, had frequently been necessitated by husbands' career moves and had predominantly involved assuming pastoral responsibilities in teaching.

CONCLUSION

This chapter has considered how policy changes in education in England in the 1960s resulted in significant shifts in career structures and promotion ladders for teachers. It would be inappropriate, however, to explain career changes as *determined* by central government and local education authority officials and/or trade union negotiators, although such macro-actors alongside media representatives clearly had a part to play in promoting and legitimating the policy changes. In effect the career and promotion ladder for teachers was changed in the 1960s and 1970s by teachers themselves. Those who recognized and anticipated the comprehensive changes were able to take career decisions to equip themselves with comprehensive experience, with pastoral responsibilities as well as curriculum management, and with the integrated subject duties which would increasingly be required for the mixed-ability pupil intakes of comprehensive schools. Some teachers would have made rational, calculating and strategic decisions to capitalize on such changes in the school and education system. Most teachers' decision-making and choices would have been shorter-term, interest-based and more idiosyncratic, however, as in particular schools, teachers' careers were developed in the changing educational contexts.

The data suggested that there were differences between men and women heads in the patterns of their career development. It has been illustrated that generally the women's promotions were slower to start. It is important also to note, however, that because of career breaks, part-time work, movements around the country in support of husbands' careers, generally the women heads' teaching experience was *wider* than that of the men heads. If the career history heads' experience is reflected more generally in teachers' careers then the different patterns of women's careers means not that they were differently equipped but that they were *better* equipped for the challenge of the new comprehensive schools. In addition to the wider extent of their teaching experience, the women heads also had more pastoral and guidance skills since more often their careers had involved head of year/house responsibilities. Again if this gender difference is more generally reflected in teachers' careers, why, in the 1970s when local education authorities were anxious to appoint managers in schools with pastoral experience, were women teachers not *better* placed than the men to become headteachers of the new comprehensive schools?

The answer is that women teachers probably were both more widely experienced and more skilled in pastoral responsibilities than their male colleagues. However, career differences between men and women do not only reflect differences in skills, talents and experiences. Gender differences in the distribution of promotion posts also reflect differences in career identity, socialization and expectation (i.e. women teachers don't apply) and differences in gender discrimination (i.e. women candidates for headship posts are more of a risk). Some of these differences are further explored in the next chapter.

Chapter 4

Applying for Headships: Continuities and Change

The process of headteacher selection is an issue of importance and interest to many, both inside and outside the teaching profession. In British secondary schools the chances of achieving a headship are small since there are relatively few such posts compared with numbers of secondary teachers. Just over 3 per cent of men secondary teachers and under 1 per cent of women are in headship posts (Acker, 1989). This chapter demonstrates that an examination of the process of selection can tell us a great deal about the role of headteacher and how that role has changed over time.

Local education authorities have had wide discretion in developing their own headteacher selection processes. They have developed procedures best fitted to the particular requirements of their areas and to the requirements of the post. Most LEAs developed standardized procedures (Morgan, Hall and Mackay, 1983) with practices varying greatly from one LEA to another, regarding such questions as who took part in selection, and the stages at which they were involved. Education officers, members of education committees and school governors were all involved, but the extent of their involvement and how influential they were in the selection proceedings depended on historical and structural constraints specific to each local authority (Smith, 1975) as well as on the personalities of the individuals involved. The headteachers in the career history study were selected under such LEA-devised procedures. Under LMS (budgetary devolution) and grant-maintained status, however, LEAs will have a reduced role and schools will operate more as autonomous and independent institutions in their selection and appointment arrangements.

The procedures involved in advertising, applying, selecting and interviewing are all part of what can be called the selection process. The variations between LEAs and some of the variations in selector roles, numbers of elimination stages, documents, activities and events used to assess candidates have been examined by Morgan, Hall and Mackay (1983), who in general were highly critical and catalogued such deficiencies as paucity of information about posts (confirmed by Free, 1984, and Owen, 1985) and inadequacy of application forms. They concluded (p. 51):

Further particulars provide incomplete information on the
school, leaving candidates guessing aspects of the school which
may be germane to their candidature. Application forms invite
candidates to provide a written statement without specification
of what it should include. Requests for references invite referees
to provide descriptions of a candidate's suitability for a post
without suggesting skill or task areas on which information is
required. The most open-ended aspect, though, is the complete
absence of a job description.

There have been attempts by some LEAs to improve selection processes by
standardizing procedures and clarifying details of posts. The interview continues to be largely unstandardized, however, and also remains critically important. Morgan and colleagues (1983, Chapter 5) have provided illuminating
illustrations of comments, views and opinions of selectors, of members of interviewing panels. This chapter will attempt to provide a counterpart, the interpretations of application and interview of some successful candidates, i.e.
current headteachers.

What is significant about the experience of application and interview? What
can we learn about institutional continuity and change from headteachers'
accounts of their candidature and selection? It is necessary to consider the
headteachers' perceptions of the procedures and practices of selection to assess
which, in their view, are the appropriate experiences and characteristics being
looked for. The selection procedures had been developed by local education
authority officers. They were then used by officers, local authority members and
governors of a school in order to select an appropriate candidate from those
applying and those shortlisted for a headship. It should be possible, therefore,
to monitor the ways in which such procedures have identified what are regarded
as positive characteristics in candidates and, by comparing long-in-post and new
headteachers, to assess how such characteristics have changed over time.

The headteachers in the career history study were post holders in two
Midlands educational authorities. The selection procedures in the two authorities were substantially different and had changed over time: changes that were
reflected in the different experiences of the older and newer headteachers. In the
group of twenty heads the age ranges of the men and women were similar. The
youngest female head was 42, the oldest 58; the youngest male head was 47,
the oldest 59. But the men had been in post longer than the women. The large
majority of the men (nine out of ten) had been heads for longer than ten years;
only one of the women had been a head for eleven years. In general, the women
had achieved their headships when they were aged forty-plus, the men when they
were in their thirties. It is also worthy of note that only two, both male,
headteachers were in a *second* headship.

In the process of application and interview, what aspects did these headteachers remember and interpret as significant in their own experiences of

selection for headship? What differences were apparent in the experiences of the long-in-post and the new headteachers? It was possible to detect aspects of both continuity and change in the selection process from the accounts the heads gave of their experiences. These aspects will be described separately.

CONTINUITIES IN THE SELECTION PROCESS

For the heads in both of the LEA counties, long-in-post and new, men and women, certain things had remained constant over time: for instance, the fortuitous, indeterminant nature of selection. Most of the group had submitted several applications, had been interviewed for some of them and succeeded eventually. The haphazard nature of the selection process emphasized by Morgan *et al.* (1983) was confirmed in these experiences. It was difficult to explain why individuals were selected for interview for some posts and not for others.

Other aspects appeared constant and stable despite stated policy objectives for change. Gender differences in the achievement of headship posts was one such feature. Both LEAs had more than eighty secondary headship posts, in one LEA eight of these posts were held by women and in the other, seven. Gender differences in promotion achievements in secondary schools continued to be highly significant. Miss Hollis, a head for eight years, described her experience of selection in the following way:

> I took about five years to persuade this authority that I was worth appointing as a head. I should think I applied for certainly a hundred jobs. I'm not bad at writing applications; I had my references taken up; I know my references were supportive. The inspectors came into the school and said 'Keep on applying, you should get there.' And I never got a sniff of an interview either in this authority or anywhere else. I mean I then had all the qualifications. I had written books. I'd had a diverse experience. I would apply and boom. So much so that I actually started to make enquiries with the Equal Opportunities Commission. I don't go through life thinking 'discrimination', women aren't going to get there; but my experience was such that there had got to be something wrong here. Nobody was saying to me well what's wrong with you is that you're short of this experience or you don't get on well with people or whatever. They were all saying you're very capable, you get on well with people, you'd make an excellent head. Blah, blah, blah, end of story. . . .
>
> So I started to think about the selection of heads and I was appalled when I started to compare notes about what had happened to friends and colleagues. I couldn't see anything consistent at all. So I wrote a paper on the subject of what

would be an appropriate system for recruiting heads and I sent this to the Director of Education. . . .

And sure enough his secretary rang me and said he would like to see me. So I went to see him and had a most civil discussion about the selection of deputies for heads, and I think that was the first time he had ever seen me. He accepted full responsibility for why I hadn't been interviewed; he said he wasn't going to hide behind the inspectors – though I actually think it was the inspectors. . . .

And interestingly, within three months, I was interviewed and I was appointed as a result of my first interview.

(Miss Hollis; a head for eight years)

The different ways in which members on selection panels regard male and female candidates for headship remained an aspect of continuity. The career history heads felt that school governors would be more reluctant than LEA officers to appoint a woman head and would regard such a candidate as more of a risk. The greater influence given to schools themselves in the selection of staff, as a result of LMS and grant-maintained status, might increase gender differences in the achievement of senior promotion posts, therefore. Discrimination is difficult to demonstrate but gender differences in headship selection experiences are an aspect of continuity rather than of change.

Other features of continuity emerged from the heads' interpretations of their experiences of the selection process. Heads referred to the networking of information about vacancies and likely candidates. They speculated about the part played by LEA officials in producing shortlists and distributing promising candidates. Also the heads explored other aspects of networking, namely, the passing on of reputations of individuals, schools and even of whole LEAs.

At that time headships were coming out in little clutches and everybody knew when they were coming up because everyone knew when someone was retiring and who was likely to be applying.

(Mrs Peters; a head for one year):

Eventually there was a whole clutch of them going and it was quite clear that there was a kind of club of us going round. I think they were playing chess in County Hall and I had visions of them sort of pushing us into various squares.

(Mrs Selby; a head for five years)

The governors wanted somebody who was going to make (the school) a different place, make it a 'proper' school again rather than this avant garde place. And I think the authority had weighted the scales against the governors in that I would not

have said any of us (the candidates) were traditionalists who
would put the clock back.

(Mrs Ince; a head for nine years)

I think it is related to the sort of valuations that authorities
have of other authorities. In those days the West Riding was a
very powerful education authority and Sir Alec Clegg as its
leader was a very powerful national figure. So in a sense there
was a recognition that there was quality in West Riding
education and its managing structures and its schools.
I think we do similar things in school. You recognize that
teacher X from school A is likely to have more of what you want
than teacher Y coming from school B. That was a key factor in
my career, no doubt about it. If you look at the pattern of
promotion of heads into particular authorities, you will see
movements from what you might call a 'generating' authority.

(Mr Bennett; a head for sixteen years)

These extracts illustrate the career history heads' interpretations of common and continuing features of the headteacher selection process. There were
examples of networking, that is, of the pooling of knowledge about vacancies
amongst candidates and also of information about appropriate candidates by
LEA officials. The extracts indicated how officials might influence shortlists
and move suitable candidates around vacancies. The accounts also illustrated a
process of what might be termed 'reputing'. In such a process the reputation
(good or bad) of a school or an LEA was attached to individual candidates,
irrespective of a candidate's own particular merits and qualifications.
In summary, the experience of these secondary headteachers indicated that
gender differences, networking, the influence of administrators, and reputing
have remained constant features of the selection process.

ASPECTS OF CHANGE: FINAL INTERVIEW QUESTIONS AND PROCEDURES

The heads' experiences of final interview were very varied and illustrated the
most significant aspects of change in the process of headteacher selection. The
procedures in the two LEAs were different. In one authority, the questions in
the final interview had changed over time, although the procedures remained
substantially the same. In the second, the procedures themselves were significantly different. These changes were reflected in the different experiences of the
long-in-post and the new headteachers.
Mr Bennett had been a head in Mertonshire for sixteen years; he was
appointed when he was aged 36. His account of the final selection process was

illustrative of the experiences of heads in both the authorities who had been long-in-post:

> The process of selection was extremely crude. The time given to it was minimal. If my memory is correct, I came here on one morning in January, not knowing the place, the school or the county. I had the morning on the usual show round of the school, lunch with the governing body and a thirty-minute interview in the afternoon, and that was it. So if you look at it as a selection process, I mean it may have been an excellent one (laughter), but I didn't question that at the time. By comparison with today's interviews for headship which are often two- and three-day affairs, with in-tray exercises, presentations and a whole range of things, I think that mine was a very crude affair.
>
> The previous head had been here (for thirty-four years), so a very long-serving, very gifted head of a particular kind. But maybe in interviewing there was a desire for change, so some of the questions were geared towards developing information about the kind of person you were and your philosophy, and how that did or did not contrast with the previous occupant. So that was a strong factor in my appointment, that I was significantly different in outlook and philosophy.
>
> I remember looking for examples of what I would term 'care' of youngsters in a pastoral sense, as opposed to academic success. I gave examples of deprived youngsters and the work I had done with them. I think I was exhibiting a particular philosophy, if you like a child-centred education which was very important in [my previous authority]. I think there was a contrast there with the previous organization and I suddenly felt I was on the right track here.
>
> (Mr Bennett; a head for sixteen years)

In this head's experience of final interview, he remembered questions about educational and personal philosophy and he responded by recounting his pastoral experiences in teaching. In his recollection, questions seemed designed to illuminate his style of educational leadership.

The experience of final selection differed, however, for the newly appointed heads. In Penns County, the thirty-minute interview procedure was substantially the same but the questions asked were significantly different. Mrs Peters had been a head for one year; she achieved her headship when she was 45 years old.

> The first question took me completely by surprise because it was about post 16 provision across the county, about which I knew hardly anything to be honest....

> And there were the set questions that one might expect.
> There was one about the impact of new legislation on governing
> bodies; there was one about the impact of GCSE and how you
> would allay parents' fears. There was something about LMS, no
> detail, just to get the feel of how you viewed the management of
> LMS, I think. Those were the three set questions and after that
> there was a free-for-all and there were lots of individual
> questions. In some ways that was more pressure because they
> came from all sides, one after the other, and they varied
> enormously. Sometimes it was difficult to detect the real point.
> There were questions about what would you do with a weak
> member of staff, what would you do with difficult children, what
> would you do with a boy who was very anxious to leave school,
> would you try and persuade him to stay until sixth form. So
> they were extremely varied and some of them were huge
> questions and some were really quite specific. So it felt quite
> intense.   (Mrs Peters; a head for one year)

From Mrs Peters' account it seemed that, in the final interview, questions
had become more specific and more focused on current legislative changes in
education. Questions designed to elucidate a candidate's educational and personal philosophy were less important than the management of educational
change and dealing with problems in schools.

In nearby Mertonshire, the final selection procedures themselves had
undergone substantial revision. The influence of the POST (Project on the Selection of Secondary Headteachers) research programme (Morgan *et al.*, 1983) was
apparent in the practices, strategies and tools now used to select headteachers
in this authority. Mrs Dexter had been a head for one year and she was appointed
at age 41. In her account, the selection procedures had been expanded and formalized, and the management of certain tasks was emphasized.

> The headship interviews all followed a pattern. In the application
> you had to write about your educational philosophy in 200
> words, then key issues in education in, I think it was, not more
> than 2,000 words, then a summary of your experiences. Then, on
> the day, you were given a folder with an in-tray exercise, part of
> which was to do the staffing structure of the school, work out
> the allowances and things. We were also given something that
> you had to do a presentation on, to the governors, and you had
> the morning to work on that and you gave the presentation in
> the afternoon.
> So we had four panels during the day. In the morning there
> was a panel where you were questioned on key issues that you'd
> identified, fifteen minutes dead. Questions thrown at you. Then
> a second panel talking about your experiences. Then in the

afternoon you were taken through your response to the in-tray
exercise and you did your presentation to the governors....

Part of the in-tray exercise was about dealing with a
suspended pupil who the governors had decided to readmit. I
didn't know it at the time but that was actually based on a
real-life situation that had happened in the school, that had
caused a breakdown between the governors and the staff. And I
must have given the right answers. I did a presentation on
community education which I'm told was the best on the day. I
felt a great rapport with the panel and I just thoroughly enjoyed
myself. I was saying things I believed in anyway.

(Mrs Dexter; a head for one year)

The practices for the selection of secondary headteachers devised by Morgan
and colleagues in the POST project were based on the procedures of executive
selection used by industry and other public services.

CHANGE AND CONTINUITY

The extracts from the headteachers' accounts illustrated aspects of both change
and continuity in the process of headteacher selection. The changes in questions
and/or in procedures at final interviews indicated fundamental alterations in
selectors' perceptions of the headteacher role over the past ten years. For
those headteachers who had been in post for about eight years or longer,
questions had appeared to the candidates to encourage them to talk of their
educational philosophies and teaching objectives. They felt they were being
asked to talk about their personal aims and objectives for schools. In contrast,
for the newly appointed headteachers, questions and procedures at final
interviews had appeared to these successful candidates to be more specific.
Questions were preoccupied with the management of change, with goal setting
and achievement, with problems and difficulties in schools and with conflict
resolution.

We can assume that such changes reflected changes in selectors' perceptions of the headteacher role. The newly appointed heads had been required to
answer questions on the management of educational change and, in one
authority, had had to complete in-tray exercises involving administrative tasks
(designing a staffing structure for the school) and conflict resolution (dealing
with a disagreement between governors and staff). Selectors were now more
interested in managerial task fulfilment and executive efficiency than in educational philosophy. The headteacher was no longer primarily an educationalist.
Amongst new headteachers the organization manager (increasingly the business
manager) and executive were of paramount importance.

However, despite such changes, there were important elements of continuity in the headteacher selection process. Gender differences in the achievement of headteacher posts continued to be very large in spite of the claimed objectives of both LEAs and teacher unions in their equal opportunities policies. I have argued elsewhere (Evetts, 1990) that changes to the headteacher role currently under way in England might result in even fewer women applying and being successful in the competition for headteacher posts. If the new headteacher is required to be competitive, efficient and accountable, developing assertive and task-centred leadership styles, then such changes to the headteacher role might prove to be unattractive to many women (as well as to many men) teachers. Such changes might exacerbate rather than decrease gender differences in the achievement of headteacher posts (see Chapter 9).

Other elements of continuity in the secondary headteacher selection process require more detailed analysis and exploration. The concept of networks and the process of networking have long been recognized and acknowledged as important in both occupational and family decisions and arrangements (Bott, 1957, 1971; Salaman, 1974; Allan, 1979). However, the significance of networks in promotion and selection processes is relatively unexamined. There is acknowledgement that networking is important but it remains a concept that is difficult to operationalize and to measure except in mathematical models of analysis.

There are similar difficulties with the concept of reputing, whereby individuals from certain schools and LEAs are assumed to have particular qualities, characteristics and attributes simply as a result of their experiences. It has been recognized for a long time that, for example, certain public school and particular university backgrounds can result in reputations and in a recognition by others of mutual allegiances and alliances (e.g. Collins, 1981). However, there needs to be further analysis of the idea of reputing and of its influence on processes of selection and promotion.

The headteachers in the career history study also speculated about the influence of LEA officials, particularly on the early stages of the secondary headship selection process. Again, there has been little systematic research on the abilities of LEA administrators and officials, of all levels, to influence educational decisions and outcomes. Morgan *et al.* (1983) did indicate the variable extent of officials powers to produce shortlists of candidates for secondary headships; and Winkley (1985) has examined the effects of LEA advisers and inspectors on promotion decisions. In general, however, we know very little about the influence of LEA officials on the selection processes for secondary headteachers.

The experience of selection for secondary headship is variable in that there are important differences over time, between different educational authorities and probably between men and women candidates. Nevertheless, analysis of such differences in experience, as well as any similarities in impressions and interpretation of selection, can increase our understanding of both change and continuity in the role of secondary headship.

It is important to recognize how the examination of individual experiences of career and promotion can alert researchers to wider organizational issues, to institutional constraints and opportunities, to structures and to processes. The separation of personal experiences from the analysis of wider socio-historical structures was a problem for earlier research. It is now recognized, however, that the relationships between identity and structure (Abrams, 1982) and the process of structuration (Giddens, 1984) necessitate the integration of experience/action and structure in investigations. A clearer appreciation of selection and appointment experiences can improve our understanding of the operation of promotion and career processes and systems.

Chapter 5

The Career and the Family: Public and Private Lives

The importance of the personal dimension in individuals' experiences of career has been neglected for a long time. The significance of personal relationships, of partnerships, marriages and families, has at last begun to be recognized by researchers (Pahl, 1984; Scase and Goffee, 1989). Indeed Scase and Goffee (1989) have argued that the personal was becoming more important than the work dimension in the career decisions of the 'reluctant' managers in their study. There have been significant gender differences in emphasis, however, in the ways in which career and family have been interrelated. When the focus of research was on men's careers, then researchers asked how far men's work responsibilities 'spiltover' (Evans and Bartolome, 1980) into the family. When women's work was studied, then the question became how far did women's family responsibilities 'spill over' into work (Rapoport and Rapoport, 1976).

The incidence of dual career couples (Rapoport and Rapoport 1971, 1976) has probably been exaggerated. Often men are able to develop what Acker (1980) called 'two-person careers' where non-working wives support their husbands' careers and take responsibility for household duties (Ball, 1987). Alternatively, the preponderance of women in routine white collar work (Rapoport and Sierakowski, 1982) means that men might be developing careers while their wives are in jobs with no formal career or promotion ladders. Even where both partners are in jobs with careers, there is a marked tendency for the man's career interests to take priority over those of the woman (Gowler and Legge, 1982). Some researchers have idealistically predicted change in this respect (Young and Willmott, 1973) and others have detected changes in women's attitudes to their work (Marshall, 1984; Scase and Goffee, 1989). However, the two-person single career is a common partnership strategy and one with which women frequently concur.

Nevertheless, the effects on men's careers of having partners with career commitments and aspirations is a growing area of interest (Rapoport and Rapoport, 1976; Rapoport and Rapoport, 1978; Rapoport and Sierakowski, 1982; Cooper and Davidson, 1982; Nicholson and West, 1988). The necessity for dual career negotiation rather than two-person single career commitment puts limitations on the man's career moves. The need for the balancing of career developments between partners becomes more critical if the partnership is to continue. It becomes necessary to examine the different ways in which 'balance' is achieved and the inherent difficulties of such balancing strategies.

This chapter examines the interrelationship between careers and personal lives of the headteachers in the careers history group. How were careers and personal relationships mutually affected and affecting and what different kinds of resolutions had been developed and experienced? Were there any gender differences in the ways in which careers and personal lives were associated and connected?

STRATEGIES

The advantages of strategic analysis (pp. 9–11) are clear in that such an interpretation of action avoids portraying actors as passive, and evades the necessity of regarding social institutions and structures as the ultimate determinants of all outcomes. However, the examination of the use of the concept of 'strategy' by Crow served to remind researchers that some actions are more usefully investigated in terms of strategies than others (Crow, 1989, p. 1). Similarly Morgan (1989, p. 28), in a comment on Crow, has argued that 'the real question is not one of whether a particular action is "really" strategic but rather the more pragmatic one of the further insights we may or may not gain from such an application'. It is necessary, therefore, to demonstrate the gains from regarding career/personal arrangements as strategies, and from the classification of such strategies.

The intellectual gains from employing the term 'strategy' in order to go beyond the classic structure/agency dichotomy are widely acknowledged. The concept of 'strategy' enables researchers to explore the interrelationship between structure and action by recognizing both the presence of structural constraints and the active responses of social actors to such constraints. Actions are no longer completely determined by social forces. Constraints are real but responses are variable. By examining strategies a crude structuralism with an implicit reification, and a simple voluntarism which neglects power and resource dimensions, can both be avoided. In the case of headteachers' careers, the constraints arising from career and personal responsibilities were real and gender differences in career and family roles were established and supported by ideologies and beliefs. But, nevertheless, the strategic management of career and personal dimensions was variable; there were different patterns of response and different ways of managing the dilemmas and the contradictions, as the accounts of the career history headteachers demonstrated.

There are other advances in theoretical understanding to be gained from the interpretation of headteachers' career and personal arrangements as strategies. Morgan (1989, p. 26) emphasized that use of the term strategy enabled a clear recognition of 'process', of how 'the analysis of household strategies is a crucial element in the understanding of processes of social reproduction and social change'. Morgan referred to Bourdieu's discussion of 'habitus' as an analysis in part of how strategies 'finally come to be seen as inherent in the nature of things' (Bourdieu, 1976, p. 118). For the headteachers, their different strategies for combining careers and personal responsibilities demonstrated the continuation of traditional patterns (single careers) which involved reproduction, and the difficulties of initiating social change (through various strategies of management in dual careers).

The paper by Crow examined at some length the issue of the actors involved in any strategic action. 'The question of whom, in the case of individuals, or what, in the case of collectivities, is being treated as the originator of a strategy is an important one' (Crow, 1989, p. 2). He then went on to explore the extent to which collectivities such as households or classes could be treated as social actors at all. His discussion of appropriate levels of analysis was linked with the question of power and he argued that where a collectivity such as a household was regarded as the locus of strategic action then this could result in the neglect of (gender) differences in influence in arriving at a household decision. Thus where researchers focus on collective action (e.g. household strategies) rather than individual decisions (e.g. the demands of the man and woman in the household) then there is a danger that the power processes behind the household action remain unexplored. This was a potential problem in the analysis and classification of the material from the career history study. It would have been possible to examine household strategies in the context of careers, since this would have linked the research with the wide variety of historical studies of family and household strategies listed by Morgan (1989). However, this might have worked to disguise some of the resource differences which men and women have in attempting to combine career and family responsibilities. Men have ideological support and confirmation for career dedication and development whereas women developing careers are path-finders in an, as yet, relatively unsympathetic and underresourced world. Thus whereas men are expected to combine career achievements with marriage and fatherhood in particular ways, women have still to develop the strategies that might eventually come to be regarded as the normal and the appropriate ways of doing such things.

The extent to which there could be 'unconscious strategies' was also considered by Crow. 'There is no set of rules forbidding the use of the term "strategy" in other ways, but normally it is taken to imply the presence of conscious and rational decisions involving a long-term perspective' (Crow, 1989, p. 19). He argued that a convention to confine use of the term strategy to conscious, rational actions allowed strategic action to be distinguished from other types, such as traditional action. With the career history headteachers, it would be possible to debate and to disagree about the conscious rationality of their career and personal strategies. What was important, however, was the blurring of the boundaries between traditional and rational action. The 'single career' strategy of the heads could be interpreted as traditional action in that continuity, reference to the past, and lack of calculation were apparent in such strategies. However, the traditional actions of individuals and couples developing single careers might be found to contain both instrumentality and rationality. It was, after all, a rational action for men careerists to develop and maintain traditional single career partnership strategies.

The appropriate term for analysis of the career/personal experiences seemed to be 'strategy', therefore, rather than the vaguer and less theoretically precise notions of actions or arrangements. This was the case even if the strategies were 'unconscious' (i.e. not calculative or long-term) since the outcomes were, nevertheless, particular kinds of career patterns with essential differences in attitudes, expectations and responsibilities. So, using the career history data, the distinctive arrangements arrived at in households in order to enable at least one person to develop a career in teaching, will be regarded as strategies. Strategies were continuously being developed and redefined as responsibilities and constraints were encountered, negotiated and managed. As problems and constraints varied over the course of careers so too did the strategies to cope with contingencies. However, career strategies were not usually clearly perceived and early formulated life plans. For most of the career history headteachers, career and personal responsibilities were in continuous process of emergence, development and management. Strategies were developed and decisions made sometimes through deliberate planning and skilfully executed tactics but, more often, strategies were devised through chance and coincidence, expectation and short-term planning, procrastination and serendipity.

Although each headteacher's career development was unique in some respects nevertheless certain patterns were discernible. Three categories of career/personal arrangements were immediately apparent, each having alternative strategies within it:

> **single career**
>> the one-person career strategy
>> the two-person career strategy
>
> **dual career**
>> postponement strategy
>> modification strategy
>> balancing strategy
>
> **marital breakdown; when partnership strategies are unsuccessful**

These different strategies will be examined and illustrated using the relevant interview data. All of the different strategies can be illustrated in this way, though clearly some strategies were more frequent than others. The numbers in each category will be given in order to indicate its popularity or rarity among the career history heads. But this was not quantitative research and such numbers cannot indicate rates of occurrence more generally.

Single Career

The single career category consists of those households where there is only one person developing a career. These might be one-person careers, as when the headteacher has remained unmarried. Alternatively, the single career might be a two-person career. In this case, one partner develops a career while the other works in the household or in an occupation with or without a career ladder but where no promotion is sought. In the career history group there were two unmarried women heads developing one-person single careers. There were no unmarried men. For Miss Reeves, the realization of what she wanted from her career was linked with her growing awareness that she would probably not get married (see p. 32). Her career strategy involved an increasing concentration on promotion and career development. But although it might seem that Miss Reeves' career strategy was unconstrained by family and personal responsibilities and that she could devote herself single-mindedly to developing her career, nevertheless she applied and eventually got her headship in an area which enabled her to be near her elderly parents. The unmarried state for women (or indeed for men) does not always mean single-minded career dedication and the total absence of family responsibilities.

The two-person single career strategy was developed by six men in the career history study; none of the women heads had pursued such a strategy. The one career and one homeworker strategy was illustrated by Mr Stevens's partnership arrangements:

> My wife trained as a junior teacher but she's only taught infants. She stopped teaching when Tony was born and she's never gone back. We decided, she decided and I certainly supported her, that she didn't want to be working because of the pressures of two people working in teaching and the pressures that puts on the family. Of course there's the money which can provide certain benefits but on the other hand we felt being together and the rest of it was more important, and her being at home.
>
> She's done a little bit of supply teaching, really since we came here. Now she's gone back as an education care officer, you know, classroom support rather than a full-time teaching job. Since last term, she's been working with a Down's Syndrome girl, who is in the mainstream school and she really loves that.
>
> (Mr Stevens)

The one career/one homeworker strategy is increasingly becoming a temporary arrangement for a particular period in the life-cycle of the family. Thus women are full-time homeworkers when the children of the couple are young. This arrangement comes to an end, however, as the children grow and gain independence. Then the homeworker returns to paid work, perhaps part-time, as Mr Stevens's wife had done. Alternatively, the woman continues in paid work, working intermittently and always prepared to move if necessary. The work of such women can be termed an occupation rather than a career since promotion ladders either do not exist or are not climbed. This is to adopt a male-defined model of career/occupation differences and it does not necessarily represent how all women (or indeed all men) experience their working lives. However, the men and women headteachers in the career history study made such a distinction so it seemed appropriate to apply it in this context.

> My wife's career is fairly routine as well. She was a secretary when we married but the first baby was born within the first eighteen months of our marriage and she stopped work when he was born.
>
> When we moved here we had our second family then and she stopped working for eleven or twelve years until our younger son was in secondary school. Then she started work again as a part-time secretary and she's worked there ever since, about ten or eleven years.
>
> You would have to ask her how she views her career but I would say she did not see her work as being central to her life with me. She was prepared to let me be the career person and she would follow. But I don't think she would give up her present job happily, because I think she likes it. She calls it her little job.
>
> (Mr Wells)

> My wife's a teacher and wherever we've lived she's taught. Her career has not been a career. She's a very experienced teacher – she's done everything from private tutoring of disturbed children, to primary teaching, to A-level.
>
> We've never really settled for very long before this stint. She did start to make a career in [_____] and was second in the English Department. But she's always been happy to move and, at present, for instance, she's just doing supply work. She has a connection with a local senior high school and they call upon her when they're short in their English Department. And well she enjoys that. . . .
>
> (Mr Lane)

Some of the problems for women who want to return to work and to a career but who find they are just too old are explained by Mr Johnson. He was also well aware of the 'empty-nest syndrome' and of the devastation to personal lives that can occur when children leave home. When children have been central to family and personal lives, any feelings of emptiness and of perceived lack of purpose and function are likely to be experienced acutely by women. Men would continue to have their careers.

[My wife] didn't work whilst the children were young but went back to part-time and temporary work as a secretary when they were at school and she did have more time. When we were living at [_____] she did temporary work again, nothing permanent. Then when we came here, we've been here now eleven years and for five or six of those years she's been working on a part-time basis, twenty-four hours per week, at a local building society, working as a secretary to the surveyor. So, in fact, she has left her languages behind, still kept her secretarial skills going and has been in the present job longer than she has spent anywhere.

She is keen to get back to her language work; concerned that she is getting a bit old now. In real terms, that is ridiculous; but in terms of perceptions and appointing practices, it isn't ridiculous.

We are both now looking ahead to the time when both our daughters will have left home. Cath's on the way now. She's spent the year off, half of it at least, working as an au pair and she will inadvertently refer to it as 'home', which stabs at the heart a bit, but she's on the way. A wonderfully loving girl, a very homely girl, somebody who it has been difficult to push out, but going to university. She's feeling anxious as lots of teenagers do I guess, but also excited, and I'm excited for her because she's going to be reading English, like her Dad did.

Our youngest daughter, Helen, is doing work experience at the moment. When I see her, like she was this morning, nervous, anxious, embarrassed about meeting people that she doesn't know in a professional situation, then my heart goes out to her as well. And it won't be long before she leaves home, she's more adventurous than Cath.

And we are looking ahead, and especially I think this is true for my wife, to when the girls have gone and the gap that that will leave in our lives. She is most keen, if not anxious on occasions, to make sure that that gap is filled before it arrives. She is anticipating the working out of that, the implications of being on our own and of her having much more time on her own than she has now. She very sensibly realises that that could be a difficult time for her, a barren period which she is anxious, keen, to fill and prepare to fill as effectively as possible. My job is fairly all-consuming anyway so I don't have that same sort of feeling. I just regret the girls going.

(Mr Johnson)

The single career partnership strategies that have been illustrated in this section might also be termed traditional household arrangements. There is one career only and hence career conflicts are absent or are minimal. It is a successful strategy, in its various forms, as long as the individuals concerned readily accept and continue to accept traditional interpretations of male and female roles. A traditional interpretation involves the separation of work and family. In traditional partnerships the male takes on the instrumental role of family provider and develops a career in part because that increases the family's wealth resources. The woman takes on the expressive role of the maintenance of family unity and stability, she supports the husband's work sometimes developing a 'wife-of' role (Finch, 1983) and, at the same time, takes responsibility for household and child-rearing duties. This traditional interpretation is maintained in the alternative single career form, where, if the woman does pursue a career, she remains single and thereby avoids some family responsibilities, although possibly still fulfilling obligations to extended family members.

Dual Career

The concept of a dual career family was first suggested and analysed by the Rapoports (1971). Since then, the idea has been re-examined (Rapoport and Rapoport, 1976) and refined (e.g. Gowler and Legge, 1982). It is usually argued that the incidence of dual career families is probably exaggerated, since in terms of strategies more families will be developing two-person single careers. Also, even if both partners are in jobs with career ladders, households in which the man's career interests always take priority over those of the woman are not dual career households. McRae (1986) demonstrated the difficulty of locating a sample of a significant size in order to study the occupational superiority of wives. In respect of careers in teaching, gender differences in promotion achievements have been highlighted. Ball (1987, pp. 197–8) has claimed that many men are able to develop two-person careers while married women are typically part of two-career families. But this is probably too simple a statement of the differences since many women teachers are in families developing two-person *single* careers, rather than dual career families. Where the husband's career takes priority, then the wife's teaching might be more accurately described as a one career/one occupation partnership rather than a dual-career household. I have confined my use of the term 'dual career' to households where both husbands and wives have sought and gained significant promotions in their careers. In the headteacher career history study the strategies developed by couples which have enabled dual career development were of three kinds:

> a *postponement strategy* involved one partner postponing career
> development until the other partner had achieved a
> significant promotion position, and then subsequently taking
> steps to develop the second career;
> a *modification strategy* in which one partner adapted a career in

order to better fit the career achievements of the other
partner;

a *balancing strategy* in which both partners attempted
complementary career development, climbing ladders and
gaining promotions simultaneously or alternatively.

The success of the three strategies in terms of the extent to which both partners
were able to develop their careers was very variable.

Postponement Strategies For the career history headteachers, the postponement strategy had been developed in four households, those of three women
heads and one man head. Mr Draper's wife had left her own career development
very late. She had achieved promotion but was unlikely to get any further
advancement in her own career:

> She was a teacher until 1959 when my son was born and then
> she had something like fourteen years of broken service while the
> children were growing up. Our daughter was born three years
> later. She did a bit of part-time just to keep her hand in. For the
> past fourteen years she has had a permanent post in a primary
> school in the village close to home. She is thoroughly enjoying it.
> She is on a scale A responsibility allowance which she got last
> year. She was in charge of the Infant Department on scale 2 but
> scale 2 was absorbed into main professional grade. But now she
> has a scale A.
>
> I am very fortunate in having her because she is happy
> teaching. I have been fortunate in being able to talk to her and
> discuss things with her. We fit our life in between our work.
>
> (Mr Draper)

Of the three women heads who had developed postponement strategies,
again it was the woman who had postponed; there were no examples of men
postponers. The three women heads had waited until their husbands were
established in their careers before developing their own careers. Mrs Morley's
dual career partnership was made up of two careers in teaching. In her household, her own career postponement enabled both partners to develop careers. An
extract from Mrs Morley's account has already appeared (p. 32). This is a more
extended version.

> My husband and I met when we were students at training
> college from 1950–52. We married in 1955 and both taught in his
> home town. He started out teaching Maths and Science at a
> secondary modern school. Then he got a job in Pennington
> teaching Religious Studies in a boys' secondary modern school
> and we moved here. He was there about five years in which time
> he got the first promotion, an A allowance. Then he moved to a

B at another boys' secondary modern school. There he was in charge of slow learners in the school. Then from that he went into special education; he got a deputy headship at a special school at [_____]. Then very quickly afterwards he got the headship of a new school for boys with behavioural difficulties. That would be Easter 1969. He was only there about two or three years and he got the headship of a special school for children with moderate learning difficulties. He's been there for seventeen years and went there when our daughter was two.

In 1974, Pennington went comprehensive and career-wise it put me in the right place at the right time. By then I had got to grips with the A level and I had proved that I could get good results in the subject, which to the head at that time meant I was a good teacher. She very much judged results and how you taught as going together. I had experience by then of secondary modern, junior, further education, bi-lateral, whereas most of the teachers at that school had experience of just grammar school. So I was given the job of welcoming in the first comprehensive year as Head of First Year which then became Head of Lower School when there were two years. Subsequently the Houghton agreement meant that we could have a second deputy and there was a deputy head pastoral job advertised which I applied for and I got. So within a few years I wasn't what I set out to be, which was Head of Religious Studies, I was deputy head of a comprehensive school.

In 1978 I made a sideways move and became deputy head of my local school. At the same time I was looking towards increasing my qualifications. From 1979 I took my BEd degree, following it by my MPhil. In terms of my family that meant particularly a very supportive husband who was prepared to look after our daughter who was still quite small and give me time and space to do the necessary work and I successfully got both degrees.

In 1985, the head of this school retired and I applied for the job and was successful.

(Mrs Morley)

As these extracts demonstrate, a career postponement for one of the part-ners is an important strategy in the realization of dual careers. It probably comes as no surprise that in the examples, it was the women who postponed while the men's careers took priority. Such a strategy could be perceived as relatively successful in that some of the women achieved a headteacher position despite delaying their career development. The career development of Mr Draper's wife was more limited, however. This must remind us of the reality of careers, which is that postponement is more likely to mean relatively modest promotion achievements for the postponing partner. Also, it seems almost inevitable at present that the postponing partner will be the woman.

Modification Strategies. One headteacher had developed a partnership strategy which had involved a modification and adaptation of the career path of one of the partners. A modification strategy can be similar in certain respects either to a postponement or a balancing strategy: it can involve delays in the career moves of one partner (hence postponement) or simultaneous or alternative moves (hence balancing). A modification strategy is distinctive, however, in that it involves at least one partner in changing careers. In Mr Hall's developing teaching career, his wife had modified and altered her own career in order to move to a different area of the country and to adapt to their changing family situation.

> When we first met my wife was working in the administration of the local hospital and just before we got married she became the personal secretary to two consultants. She remained doing that until the birth of our daughter. My wife's parents were alive at that time and so they were quite willing to look after our daughter. But I don't think women who took only maternity leave had their jobs kept open in the same way as now.
>
> So my wife started to work part-time, a lot of it in the evenings, again working for the local health authority, helping to run clinics. It was from there that she started to work for Social Services, again on a part-time basis, as a home help organizer....
>
> With changes in the Service they decided that home helps had to be trained and my wife was asked to involve herself with a senior colleague in a training programme. Those training programmes were put on in the local College of Further Education but run by Social Services staff and my wife was one of the staff who went to do that.
>
> About eighteen months later the college took over that training and they recruited my wife to go and work for them and they offered her more and more hours. She had trained previously to teach cookery in Further Education, although the qualification does not allow her to teach in a school [laughter]. She started in the college teaching cookery and working with pre-nursing and nursing groups, O level and A level classes as well.
>
> And that is the stage when [I got headship promotion and] we decided to come and live here. When we came here she looked at the local college here but that type of work was not available because the work they did was in catering and her qualifications were in domestic cookery really.

And that was the end of my wife's career as such. We came
to Mertonshire, bought a house and I suppose about fifteen
months later my son was born. So that didn't help my wife to
rebuild her career because knowing no one in the area she said
she had better stay at home and make sure he's alright.

Since then of course as he got a bit older, she has done lots
of things. She works in Adult Education as a part-time lecturer.
She also does a lot of voluntary work as well. . . .

Currently she is being asked by more and more people to
cater for them, for parties and things like that, again arising out
of the fact she is involved with cookery. It looks as though with
a friend of hers they could go into business in a big way. But I
don't know if they want to do it in a big way. I think they just
want something to pass the time.

(Mr Hall)

A modification strategy can be relatively successful to the extent that one
career can be pursued and the other purposefully changed and significantly
maintained. In the example above, Mr Hall's wife was able to redirect her career
several times and was able to establish an alternative, if different, career. It is
possible, also, to conceive of other modifications. If career negotiations become
more common than single career dedication amongst dual career couples, then
career modification of one or both partners might become a more frequent
strategy. Currently, however, it seems it is predominantly one partner, the wife,
who modifies.

Balancing Strategies. A balancing strategy involves both partners in attempting complementary career development, in which both climb promotion ladders
simultaneously or alternately. This is perhaps the most difficult of the dual
career management strategies to achieve. It is particularly difficult when both
partners are in the same career since direct comparisons can be made. It is a
slightly easier strategy where partners are in different careers since then direct
comparisons, other than in salary terms, are not appropriate or relevant.
Attempts to achieve balances in career development are fraught with difficulties, however, and attempts at balance might ultimately result in postponement or modification strategies. Two of the women headteachers had attempted
balancing strategies. Mrs Green's account catalogued some of the difficulties of
attempting to achieve balance in career developments. Such difficulties were
magnified when both partners were in the same career and when the more successful partner was the woman.

In his first job he taught Geography, Maths and English, I
think, in a boys' secondary modern school. He welcomed
comprehensivization and the amalgamations because that gave
him more opportunities. His career has been much less successful

61

than mine, much more frustrating for him. I was ahead of him because I was three years ahead anyway, and by teaching French I had the advantage over a geographer because geographers have always been ten-a-penny compared with linguists. Also I was coming up through the boom years, you know, more money, more teachers, more pupils. So I just sailed through internal promotions to a Head of Department's job. Martin had the opposite experience.

When Martin's friend and colleague at school, Peter, got his deputy headship, Martin thought he would be in line for Peter's job. Peter had been a scale D because he was Head of Geography, in charge of sixth form and Head of Social Education. Martin had been very heavily involved in working with Peter, they had coordinated Social Education together. Martin was already on a B for a pastoral role, head of a half year. So there was a chance of promotion at long last, if not to a D then to a C. And the head split the jobs. Martin was the only person in the school who could have taken over Geography and Social Education, there was nobody else. But the head split the jobs and they were both B's. Martin decided that if he could only get one he'd prefer Social Education. So he didn't get any more money and he certainly got more work for being in charge of Social Education. But that regenerated him. He now had something, a distinct area of the curriculum that was his, that he could work on and manage the staff, so he came through. And that took him on for the next few years.

When I got my deputy headship, that limited him to Penns County. He had come to terms with the situation he was in. He'd realized that he was not going to get a promotion out of school. That he'd been in the same school too long, he was getting too old, and realized the leap into deputy headship was gone. Along the way he did get a C out of a restructuring so he felt honour was satisfied, he'd got a promotion. Then last year he got a tourism qualification and that reawakened in him the thought that there was more to life than teaching.

He had a very tough time when I became head because it coincided with his head retiring. When the head retired, a deputy whom Martin really respected and liked became acting head. But after a second round of interviews they didn't appoint him and he eventually got a headship elsewhere. So Martin had lost his friend and mentor from the hierarchy; he'd got a new head coming in, an unknown quantity, who when he came started to make drastic changes; he'd got me in the throes of headship, and he found it all extremely stressful. So in the end he decided that

this was a good time to go. He resigned at Easter. He's become a
tourist guide and gone into partnership with a driver guide.

(Mrs Green)

A balancing strategy for dual career partnerships was slightly easier where
the partners were in different occupations each with their own career ladders for
promotion positions. Mrs Peters' account of her early career promotions is
already given (p. 37). This later extract from her account illustrated balancing,
of each partner making career moves alternately, while the other partner was
temporarily career stable. There were elements of postponement in Mrs Peters'
career but in general her career and that of her huband developed together, both
were interrelated and interdependent and both were reliant at times on the
stability of the other.

> Then when he had finished his PhD he got a job with a firm of
> consulting engineers in [_____]. This was about 1975. I then
> had another baby with maternity leave. By 1976 he was unhappy
> with the job he'd got and he got a job in Pennington and he tried
> travelling but it clearly wasn't going to work. So in the summer
> of 1976 we moved here. I was looking for a job again and it was
> really by chance that I got the job in [_____]. I had applied
> for a Head of Special Needs job, didn't get it, left my coat there,
> went back to get my coat, got lugged into a room by the head
> and offered a job in the English Department.
>
> Now [my husband] was actually with the same company
> from '76 until recently. He had various promotions and
> developments while he was there. But he has now left [that
> company] and is back in consultancy engineering. Again it's a
> development for him, it's a promotion.
>
> I stayed at that school until 1985. During that time I moved
> from a scale 2 which was for lower-ability English and Special
> Needs to a scale 3, Head of Year, fourth and fifth year, which
> was a very large group at the time, 360 children. I did that for
> about a year and a half and then I was offered a Head of Faculty
> job on a D, a 4, a Head of Guidance Faculty and putting PSE on
> the curriculum. I agreed to do that although I also had a baby
> that year as well. I did that for three years. In 1985 I got a
> deputy headship at [another school] a pastoral job. I stayed there
> for three and a half years and then I applied for this job and
> got it.

(Mrs Peters)

Balancing was, then, perhaps the most difficult of the dual career management strategies to achieve. Mrs Green's account demonstrated some of the
difficulties of attempting to achieve balance where both partners were in the

same career and the more successful partner was the woman. Mrs Peters' account illustrated balancing where the partners were in different occupations.

As all of the above accounts illustrated, in dual career partnerships, the management of careers could be done in a number of different ways. The career history headteachers had used postponement, modification and balancing strategies as ways of containing potential or actual career conflicts. Both men and women headteachers had used postponement of the woman's career development as a way of managing dual career progression. A modification strategy in this case by the wife had been developed in the household of one male headteacher. However, the potential of modification strategies is probably large, and increasing career negotiation in dual career partnerships might result in expansion and development of modification strategies perhaps for both partners. Balancing strategies were inherently difficult to manage particularly where both partners were pursuing the same career. Perceptions of balance might vary anyway and experiences of balance are subject to different interpretations.

Marital Breakdown

When partnership strategies fail marital breakdown might be the result. Both two-person single career and dual career strategies might be perceived as unsuccessful by one or both of the partners and the outcome might be separation and the ending of the partnership. In the career history study five of the headteachers, three women and two men, had experienced marital breakdowns. The two men had remarried and were developing second partnership strategies. Of the three women, one had remarried and the other two were currently developing strategies for one-person single careers. Mrs Grainger had divorced and remarried. Mrs Dexter had divorced and was single.

> My former husband is a nuclear physicist of some talent and when we married we had a great deal in common. . . . The trouble was, though, we were both so career-orientated that we stopped ever meeting. We never fell out or rowed or anything like that. Even at the time when we decided that we would separate there was never acrimony or any nastiness, we just didn't meet. We reached a point where we'd have to write notes to each other. He was moving inexorably up the ladder of [a nuclear engineering company] and a very skilled sportsman, played badminton and tennis for the county. And I was similarly moving my way up the education tree and worked very hard in the theatre.
>
> He was offered a directorship at [_____], where we started off, at exactly the time when I was applying for headships and getting the sort of feedback which suggested I was going to get one. My son was just about to go to university and there isn't a

theatre within a hundred miles of [_____]. And it didn't occur
to him that I wouldn't just go. So I had to decide that I was
going to have to say it. I was very sorry....

My current husband I got to know through our theatre
work. And I have the real advantage of managing to find a
husband who's actually really good at the things I'm not very
good at....

And he's a very great surprise because my first husband was
urbane and charming and clever but certainly had a perception
that a woman's job was to run the home. It's a bonus to find a
charming man who doesn't actually think that.

(Mrs Grainger)

In a sense I think [my former husband] would partly blame my
career and my ambition. I would say I've never been particularly
ambitious but I've always had a lot of drive and energy and I
liked being involved with things.

Anyway I got married and at first there was no problem
because we both worked at the same school. It didn't matter how
long I worked, how late, because we were coming home together
and going to school together. But once I was a deputy and I was
coming home at different times, Paul couldn't really cope with it.
It got to the point when he never knew when I was going to be
in or how long I was going to spend in my job and all the rest of
it. And I think he never realized how important my job was to
me. I mean all the things like children, we'd talked about having
children; I'd always said I didn't want to have children and he
said that's fine. Then there was a point in the relationship when
he said well I know you said you don't want to have children but
I thought if one came along then it would be OK. And I sort of
had to live with the guilt, you know, and his parents wanting us
to have children.

Then he got under pressure in his job. He took on extra
responsibilities without getting paid and then other people got
promoted around him. There was a lot of bitterness and
resentment building up about the way he was being treated. And
I took a lot of that pressure and began feeling guilty about my
success against his lack of success.

In the end I couldn't cope with the way he was dealing with
his stress which was basically to come home at night and go
over and over everything that was going on at school. I stopped
talking about my job. I wasn't getting any support from the
partnership....

He couldn't cope with my success against his lack of success, although it's never worried me. I always said to him it wouldn't worry me if he stayed a Head of Department for the rest of his life as long as he was happy, if it was what he wanted. I wasn't worried about him being what I was, we were different people. So in that sense my career didn't help. But I think there was also something about me. Maybe we didn't know each other well enough. Maybe we hadn't got the agenda properly sorted out before we went into marriage. And I think that anybody else would have to accept that my job is a very big part of my life.

(Mrs Dexter)

These two extracts illustrate a number of different features. Both the women had experienced changes in their partnership strategies. Mrs Grainger had changed a dual career balancing strategy for a dual career modification strategy in that her second husband had entered teaching after their marriage and after twenty-one years working in industry. Mrs Dexter had changed a dual career strategy which had failed to achieve balance, for a one-person single career. In addition, the two extracts demonstrate gender differences in the way in which ambition and a heavy workload are regarded. Thus, although it is entirely appropriate for men to be single-minded in their career dedication and to spend long hours at work, it is less acceptable for women to be so occupied. When women are heavily involved in their careers, then strains in the partnerships can result, unless realization of the discrepancy and an acknowledgement of the double standard as it relates to career dedication, enables couples to resolve such conflicts.

CONCLUSION

In this chapter the career and personal strategies of the secondary headteachers have been classified into three main types: single career strategies, dual career strategies and strategic failure, which involved a change to a different strategy or a different personal arrangement. From the career history research it is possible to hypothesize certain gender differences in respect of career/personal strategies, although any generalizations would need to be tested on larger samples. The one-person single career might be more a female than a male strategy since, certainly in teaching, the spinster headteacher is more common than the bachelor head. In contrast, the two-person single career is probably a male rather than a female strategy. Thus, although it is common for wives to support their husbands' careers, it is, as yet, rare for husbands to support their wives' careers.

Similarly in dual career partnerships, postponement is a popular strategy but it is more often the female who postpones rather than the male. Career modification might be becoming an increasingly popular partnership strategy and although it has probably been more common for women to be the modifiers, this might change as more women achieve significant promotions which require their partners, or both partners, to adapt their career plans. Balancing is a particularly hazardous career/partnership strategy to achieve, particularly where both partners are in the same career and direct comparisons can be made. A balancing strategy might be easier where the partners are in different careers, but perceptions of balance and experiences of balancing are likely to vary widely from one couple to another. In addition, balancing might also require important elements of career postponement and modification by one or both of the partners if such a strategy is to succeed.

Experiences of marital breakdown are probably increasing and, in part, reflect the failure of career/partnership strategies for both men and women. It is possible, however, to hypothesize that career men are more inclined than career women to seek a second partner in order to develop another partnership or another strategy. Career women might also develop a second partnership but some women are content to pursue a one-person single career strategy following the failure of a partnership strategy.

It can be argued that 'strategy' is an appropriate theoretical concept to use in the examination and analysis of career/personal arrangements in households. As the previous discussion of the concept of strategy (pp. 9–11; 51–53) made clear, an analysis of strategies enables researchers to explore the interrelationship between structures and action by recognizing both the reality of structural constraints and the active responses of social actors to such constraints. Actors have different resources, including power and cultural resources, and some of the differences are gender-related. The difficulty of interpreting 'unconscious' strategies as strategic remains and the dividing lines between rational, traditional and affective actions are not easy to draw. Particularly in the case of households and partnerships, traditional and affective actions can be interpreted as both rational and strategic for at least one of the partners. However, the most important advantage to be gained from using the concept of strategy is the emphasis that is thereby placed on the idea of process. We are able to recognize more easily how strategies are crucial to the processes of both reproduction and social change. For the headteachers in the career history group, their strategies for combining careers and personal relationships demonstrated both the continuation of traditional patterns (single careers) which involved reproduction, and, at the same time, illustrated the difficulties of initiating social change (through the various dual career strategies). The pragmatic test, of whether further insights are gained from use of the term strategy, can be demonstrated.

If there are several advantages to be gained from interpreting career/personal arrangements as strategies, then it is important to conclude, as do both Crow (1989) and Morgan (1989), with the main disadvantages. Crow ended his paper with a reminder that Foucault (1980) argued powerfully against studying strategies and Crow endorsed the objection that strategic analysis might be used to emphasize choice and to play down constraint. Morgan's objection was different. He argued that 'the use of the term "strategy" to cover a wide if indefinite range of human activity may seem to surrender too much to the forward march of rational calculation' (Morgan, 1989, p. 29). This could constitute an important comment on the interpretation of career and personal arrangements as strategies. In the examination and classification of career arrangements as strategies there was no mention of affectual or of moral action. This must be strange when the objective was to link the personal dimension with the world of work and career. The strategies analysed, which covered partnership relations between husbands and wives and sometimes by implication family relations between parents and children, included no analysis of how affection or notions of morality (the right and the good) might have influenced the strategies. Morgan warned that a strategy approach was in danger of diminishing and rendering marginal, questions of morality in actions and in researchers' understandings of action. He concluded: 'the ethical consequences of the development of a "strategies" approach are certainly double-edged, with the potential for both the enrichment and the diminishment of our moral understanding of human agency' (Morgan, 1989, p. 29).

Chapter 6

Being a Headteacher: Management Structures in Comprehensive Schools

In recent years there has been a great increase in the literature on the organization and management of schools. In England the growth in numbers of large comprehensive schools together with more recent developments such as LMS and the option of grant-maintained status have resulted in heightened awareness of the importance of management in educational establishments. Some of the literature has been theoretical in orientation (for example, the Open University Readers; see Bush, 1989) and some writers have emphasized the practical considerations of running a complex organization (Lyons and Stenning, 1986; Adams, 1987). Indeed, the gap between the theory and the practice has been a frequent cause of concern and comment (Hughes, 1986), particularly from headteacher managers themselves. This chapter will use headteachers' own accounts of the management structures in their schools as a basis from which to demonstrate the theoretical importance of how we account for and explain the nature of organization and of management of schools. The consequences of headteachers' structures of management for teachers' careers will also be considered.

The development of theory in educational management has been charted by Hughes (1986) and the distinction between organization theory and management theory has been clarified (Bush, 1989). The linkage also remains important, however, since 'management theory is grounded in organization theory which in turn has implications for management practice' (Bush, 1989, p. 4). Bush justified the importance of organization theory by arguing that an appreciation of theoretical alternatives enables managers 'to make a more accurate diagnosis of the problem and fit the responses to the situation' (p. 9). The examination of organization theory in this chapter is different, however. The intention is to examine headteachers' own accounts of the realities of organizational life in schools. The focus is heads' powers to influence managerial and organizational arrangements and hence the importance of heads' actions in reproducing or changing career structures and processes in teaching. In order to examine the extent of their powers it was important to listen to headteachers themselves talking about their management systems and how they came to operate with particular structures of management.

ORGANIZATION THEORY AND MICRO-POLITICS IN SCHOOLS

When schools have been examined using organization and management theory, a contrast is often drawn between two ideal-type models of authority. Hoyle (1986, p. 33) summarized the main differences. In a hierarchical model, authority is based on 'office' and orders are passed down through the hierarchy. As far as the school is concerned, this means a high degree of authority is vested in the head and transmitted through heads of departments/years. Importantly, though, such a model talks of the head's *authority*, thereby implying consensus and agreement about heads' abilities to direct the management of their schools without disagreement or opposition. In the second ideal-type, in a collegial model, authority is located in the groups of professional equals who govern their affairs by democratic procedures. In respect of the school, policy is decided by an academic board in which teachers participate on a democratic basis. The collegial model also discusses the *authority* of the professional and by implication assumes consensus on educational goals and means. Hoyle suggested that much of the discussion about schools as organizations had been couched in terms of the two models as alternative organizational arrangements. There was a normative preference for the collegial system since schools were organizations of professionals. Professionals, it could be argued, flourished in and preferred collegial systems of authority. Hoyle concluded, however, that this was far too simple a statement of how schools were organized and managed (p. 49). In fact neither hierarchical nor collegial models were 'better' or 'worse' and either could be appropriate in certain contexts and some mix of the two in other contexts.

The main problem, according to Hoyle, was that there was as yet too little empirical research to specify what mix would be effective for schools under what conditions. It might be the case, however, that the conceptualization of the problem in terms of alternative *authority* patterns was misleading. Ball (1987) has argued that organization theorists have concentrated on authority and in so doing have assumed that authority is accepted, and consented to and that, as a consequence, conflict over organizational decisions is pathological and unusual. Instead, Ball has suggested that a theory of school organization should analyse the micro-politics of school life, that is the various ways in which power is exercised in schools. Thus, instead of assuming consensus and legitimacy at the outset, such an analysis would expose the interpersonal influences, the compromises and the negotiations that are part of work in schools. Such an analysis would demonstrate how power is exercised, how it is reinforced and reproduced sometimes as a result of conflict and struggle but also through mechanisms of acceptance and legitimacy. Similarly, such an analysis could indicate how reproduction or change in structures and processes in schools are brought about by heads and by teachers themselves.

Micro-political analysis is a relatively new initiative in sociological and educational research. It represents an attempt to combine the analytical strengths of two theoretical strands: first, that of interactionist theory and ethnographic methods which have concentrated on actors' meanings, experiences and interpretations of events (e.g. Woods, 1983; Burgess, 1985b, 1985c) and have the advantage of concentration on detail and reporting events how they were. Second, that of organization theory itself, which has developed models of organizations as abstract operational systems and has examined the strengths and weaknesses of different organizational arrangements (Turner, 1968; Hoyle, 1975; King, 1983; Bush, 1989). The political dimension of organizations, particularly in respect of schools, has not always been sufficiently developed, according to Ball (1987). He suggested that studies of schools as organizations had assumed that the authority of the head was always accepted unquestioningly and that heads' decisions went unchallenged. Clearly this was far too simple an interpretation of events in schools, as headteachers widely recognized. In fact, authors such as Hoyle (1982, 1986) had always emphasized the power dimension in schools, particularly in respect of the relations between heads, other managers and classroom teachers.

In answer to the question how are schools organized, Ball has argued 'that they are places where interpersonal influence, compromise and behind-the-scenes negotiation are as important as formal procedures and official meetings' (1987) cover-sheet. Following his suggestion, it could be more fruitful to analyse headteachers' uses of power in organizing their schools rather than assuming at the outset that they use their authority in different ways under different conditions to determine the schools' management arrangements.

This chapter takes a first step in this direction by demonstrating the extent of the powers heads have in influencing the management systems in their schools. In turn this will give some indication of the extent of heads' abilities to introduce changes in the career structures and processes for teachers in their schools. It also demonstrates certain aspects of the work culture of headship, of heads' experiences and what it means to be a headteacher. Obviously heads are only one of the participants in micro-political activities in schools. Other managers and teachers also have bargaining powers and spheres of influence in negotiations. Nevertheless, heads have greater power resources compared with other staff. The intention is not to portray heads as demagogues since this would be far too simplistic and too crude a representation. It is rather to portray headship as a strategic performance in which heads exercise political skills in devising managerial arrangements in their school organizations. This would seem more productive of explanations of how things really are in schools. Such a model explores what it means to be a headteacher and recognizes heads' everyday experiences of organizational life.

In addition to collecting information about their career histories, the heads in the career history study were asked about the management structures in their schools: how they organized their staff; how tasks and responsibilities were divided up and distributed among and between posts. In other words, the heads were asked to explain their structures of management and how their schools were run. This chapter begins by exploring the limits and constraints on headteachers' powers to devise systems of management. It then examines the extent of manoeuvrability which heads have in developing alternative managerial arrangements. Extracts from the headteachers' accounts are used to demonstrate both the limits to and the extent of their powers.

INFLUENCES ON MANAGEMENT SYSTEMS

From the headteachers' accounts, it became clear that there were two main influences on the construction and development of management systems in schools, two main constraints on their organizational arrangements. The first was the national salary structure for teachers in England, which is also the career and promotion ladder for the profession. This structure was perceived as both enabling and constraining: enabling in that the structure provided a framework within which heads could promote and reward teachers for taking on additional administrative and managerial responsibilities; constraining in that it limited the diversity of management structures it was possible to devise in schools. The second influence was the need to incorporate and accommodate educational changes. Adjustment to educational change has been a constant feature of managers' tasks in schools but certain aspects of recent legislation in England, together with demographic changes, were likely to have a direct impact on management structures themselves. As with the national salary structure, educational change could be enabling as well as constraining on heads' development of management arrangements. These two kinds of influence will be examined separately and illustrated using extracts from the headteachers' accounts.

Career and Salary Structure

The career and salary structure for the teaching profession in England has been subject to modification and development. Until 1987 the salary structure and the promotion ladder for teachers, the Burnham scales, were devised nationally as a result of negotiation between teachers' unions and the employers' representatives, the local education authorities. Governments exercised a restraining influence. The Burnham scales were altered and adjusted in 1956 and 1971 (Hilsum and Start, 1974). Then in 1987, the Secretary of State for Education abandoned the Burnham scales and disbanded the negotiating machinery. The complex structure of four salary scales for teachers was replaced by a Basic Scale plus a system of Incentive Allowances (A–E) for teachers taking on additional responsibilities. Teachers' national negotiating rights were held in abeyance (for three years) and local differences in pay, particularly in areas of teacher shortage and for teachers of shortage subjects, began to be developed more extensively.

The organizational structures of management in schools are greatly influenced and constrained by the system of salary and promotion scales. Differences in salary do not only, or even mainly, reflect differences in length of teaching experience or quality of teaching expertise. Differences in salary have come to be identified with management. The salary structure which provided the career development ladder for individual teachers came to be totally associated with management tasks and responsibilities. The 1971 Burnham settlement included an agreement to drop the assumption that promotion would necessarily involve the acceptance of additional administrative responsibility (Saran and Verber, 1979). But this has not affected promotion patterns. In the organization of secondary schools in England, virtually every allowance involves some management/administrative responsibility (West-Burnham, 1983).

All maintained secondary schools in England have management systems to organize and delegate curriculum, pastoral and administrative responsibilities. There are variations both in form and in detail but the most common kind of managerial organization of posts and responsibilities, influenced greatly by the salary and promotion structure, is some variant of that described by Mr Draper:

> I have three deputy heads, one is curriculum, one is pastoral and one is day-to-day. The curriculum deputy is male and he is looking after National Curriculum development. The pastoral deputy is male and he looks after active tutorials and records of achievement. The day-to-day deputy is female and she looks after the timetable and LMS. We have three senior teachers on Es. One man who is associated with the curriculum deputy who looks after the family of schools, in-service training and helps with the development of the National Curriculum. We have one woman who is associated with the pastoral deputy who looks after records of achievement and coordination with primary schools. The third senior teacher is associated with the day-to-day deputy and deals with maintenance of buildings, caretakers, and that is a woman.
>
> We have heads of departments and heads of faculties. Somewhere round about the eight hundred pupils mark, the departmental system appears to start breaking down with meetings of twenty-plus department heads and needs the injection of another tier of management so that policy can be kept to, in terms of the dissemination into the departments. So I instituted a faculty system with faculty heads on Ds, and that formed quite a nice group of people. The chairman of the curriculum group (of faculty heads) is the curriculum deputy.
>
> Then we have six years in the year system. We have two year-heads per year (one on a C and one on an A or B depending on their other responsibilities) except for the sixth form where we have got one, so that is eleven. They form the pastoral committee which is chaired by the pastoral deputy. We have now

got a resource committee which looks at the resources of the school in terms of LMS and is chaired by the day-to-day deputy.

In the faculties we have roughly equal groups of teachers, about ten per faculty. They are split up into departments and some are obviously larger than others but the faculties seem to be roughly equal at about ten or twelve. The year heads have between seven and ten tutors. They have year meetings with the two year heads to about seven to ten tutors. These teachers are on allowances to the extent they have a whole school responsibility.

(Mr Draper; head of group 11 school)

This account illustrates what is perhaps one of the most common systems of management in secondary schools in England. Such an organization of posts and positions and such a delegation of tasks and responsibilities is strongly influenced by the national career and salary structure which sets the limits and indirectly regulates the allocation of responsibilities and allowances. This account represents what has been called a hierarchical structure of authority (Hoyle, 1986, p. 33), in which authority is based on 'office' and orders are passed down through the hierarchy and transmitted through deputies, heads of departments/years and so on. Such a management structure has numerous, widely acknowledged, advantages. Levels and areas of responsibility and accountability are clear and easily understood. The boundaries and limits of responsibility are defined so that the particular functions of individual teachers are identified and widely known. By these means, delegation can be effective and communication, as long as it goes upwards as well as downwards, can avoid some of the potential difficulties of bureaucratic impersonality.

In devising and developing management systems, heads have to make use of the salary and promotion ladder. In organizing and allocating a division of tasks and responsibilities, and in rewarding those undertaking such responsibilities, heads are both enabled and constrained by the salary and promotion structure. The number of promotion allowances available in a school has been determined in the past by an LEA formula in which the most important factor was the size of the school, in particular a school's unit total. With the development of LMS, however, heads together with their governors will have more influence in determining the number and distribution of promotion allowances in their schools and any LEA formula will constitute a guide rather than a limit. The *distribution* of promotional allowances, however, in contrast to the number, has always been a matter for negotiation between individual heads in consultation, to varying extents, with their management teams and governors. It is this influence over the distribution of promotion posts which gives heads manoeuvrability and power in devising what are essentially their own systems of management. In determining the distribution of management posts, heads are constrained by two additional factors. The first is the notion of what is 'common practice' in that what other heads do/have done comes to constitute a norm which forms the basis for teachers' and others' expectations. Secondly, heads are constrained by an inherited pattern of management when they take over in an established school. The legacy of an operational management system can limit a head's manoeuvrability in numerous ways and for long periods of time.

Educational Change

In England change is a constant feature of the educational system and of educational establishments such as schools. Research into the management of change in schools is relatively new, however, despite changes in education – both large-scale (for example, comprehensivization) and smaller-scale (school amalgamations) – over recent years. There is a need to explore the different ways in which schools cope with and respond to changes in educational tasks and goals, changes in local educational authority relations and responsibilities, and changes in a school's situation brought about by alterations in numbers of pupils on roll.

In addition, in the 1980s there has been educational legislation in England which has brought a shift in relations between schools and parents and between schools and local education authorities. Education Acts in 1987 and 1988 initiated progress towards a national compulsory curriculum, towards local management of schools (LMS) and increasing parental choice of schools. Also, during this period, demographic change resulted in a declining number of pupils in schools, which precipitated the need for reorganization and rationalization in many local authority areas. These changes have to be managed by headteachers and incorporated into their management structures. The consequences for management teams are significant: they have to be responsive and demonstrate flexibility, and management structures frequently have to be rationalized so as to complete tasks and goals, often without additional resources and rewards. In some cases, as with declining school rolls, management has to incorporate change with a reduction of resources.

The impact of such educational changes in England has influenced heads' construction and development of management structures and has increased the amount of micro-political negotiations in schools over tasks and responsibilities. Some changes were perceived as constraints by the career history heads. A reduction in size of school (unit total) provided a smaller number/amount of promotion allowances for distribution among staff. In addition, most heads inherited a management structure that involved certain teachers in post, or redeployed teachers, being on protected salaries. This could severely constrain manoeuvrability in altering the management systems. Also, the balance in any one school between static and mobile teachers could affect the development of management structures for long periods of time. These constraints on heads' ability to change management were likely to be more strongly felt as a result of LMS.

Change could also enhance heads' opportunities to develop management positions, however. Enhanced opportunities would in turn increase micro-political activity in schools over managerial structures, as some of the accounts demonstrated. Mr Stevens had had to manage a school with a declining roll and the legacy of a top-heavy management structure with large numbers of teachers in high promotion positions. The decline in pupil numbers had been reversed and he was beginning to manage an expansion in numbers. He was well aware of the increased flexibility such expansion gave him in his micro-political negotiations with teachers over promotion allowances.

There's myself and two deputies. One is essentially pastoral, you know, pupil care and guidance, relations with parents, monitoring of pupils. He's got a lot of other tasks as well like the school calendar and a host of things like that. The other deputy is curriculum and staffing. When I had three deputies I really had the pupil deputy, a curriculum deputy and a staffing deputy. I ran it like that and I tended to deal with the finance. With losing that third deputy, the staffing is the one that tends to get divided up now.

I've got no Es and that's historical. What I inherited here was a tremendous number of staff on D's or the equivalent at that time. It was a very top heavy structure and a whole load of staff on nothing. Young staff that were coming into the school really had very little incentive to stay, and I've tried to alter that. So on a D I have a management assistant, very much a day-to-day school administrative type of job. I've got the community tutor who is very much a member of the senior management . . . and the community dimension to the school is quite extensive. I've also a head of upper school who has a wide brief in terms of careers education and industry links. I've got a staff development coordinator and a resources manager. All of those people are on a D. They're not on a D solely for those jobs. If you take the staffing coordinator, he in fact is Head of English and he had his D because he was Head of English. He does the other job because he wants to, he wants to be involved in the management of the school. But he's not going to get any more for doing it because the way I've worked that one is that he stays on a D but a lot of his work as Head of English is now done by the number two in English. She is a young, very enthusiastic teacher with tremendous potential and I've managed by all sorts of means to get her on a B.

Then in middle management I've tried to move towards the faculty structure and a block timetable. I've tried to group subject areas where I can into faculties and I've gone for heads of faculties although some won't fit in so they remain heads of department. I want the faculty heads all on Cs, that's what I'm aiming for and that's what the governors have agreed. There are one or two for historical reasons that are on Ds. I inherited a situation where Head of Creative Studies, CDT Faculty was on a D and Head of Maths was on a B. Now Head of Creative Studies Faculty, stays on a D but I've managed to get Head of Maths on to a C as numbers have gone up slowly, but it's been a difficult process. I've had to use every penny I've got in order to reach this structure. I've still got two heads of faculty on Bs but hopefully within a year I will be able to put them up to Cs.

Then the other side, the pastoral side, I've got a team of heads of year. They are now all on Bs. They've got that for being heads of year and that job has got more and more demanding. But they're also delivering the PSE taught curriculum and also between them they're taking on most of the coordination of the National Curriculum. So they've got quite a big job there but it's not just a pastoral job and I was keen to add this curriculum dimension. I think it's good for them to have the crossover between the curriculum and the pastoral sides. It gives them a better appreciation and they will be working with colleagues from curricula areas in developing these cross curricula themes. Hopefully I've got it right; time will tell.

I've got a lot more manoeuvrability now with incentive allowances, much more flexibility. It gives me a lot of satisfaction when it all adds up to a particular person getting an allowance, which I know they've earned for the last three years. In the next couple of years it will get even better as our numbers go up. I don't intend to be a head who saves on incentive allowances. I'm going to use it all and more if I can get it for staff. They are the greatest resource in the school.

(Mr Stevens; head of group 8 school)

This account illustrates a number of the constraints and opportunities of educational change which limit and give options to heads in devising their management teams. The movement of staff, usually for promotion, and the allocation of allowances, for example, constituted an opportunity for micro-political negotiation. The amalgamation of posts, positions and responsibilities in order to economize on expenditure, limited the opportunities for junior teachers to begin to climb the promotion ladder by taking on small amounts of managerial responsibility and was also likely to result in an increase in micro-political activity between heads and their teaching staffs. The stability or, in particular, the reduction in promotion allowances available to schools, for whatever reason, resulted in post-holders being required to fulfil numerous responsibilities sometimes without corresponding promotion or with no promotion at all. The powers of the head in organizing such rationalizations would be a highly productive topic of research using micro-political theory. The dangers inherent in such economies or rationalizations have been described by West-Burnham (1983). Mr Stevens' account also illustrated the importance of expansion of pupil numbers for increasing the manoeuvrability of heads and enlarging the amount of micro-political negotiations in schools in devising what heads saw as appropriate management (and hence career) structures.

CHANGING MANAGEMENT STRUCTURES

The national career and salary structure for the teaching profession is a critically important influence on and determinant of the management systems in schools. Heads are both enabled and constrained by this structure in terms of the management arrangements they can devise. Similarly, educational change and the need to respond to changing situations also limit and extend heads' opportunities in respect of their management systems. The accounts of the career history headteachers demonstrated that there was considerable room for manoeuvre. The heads could and did respond differently to the constraints and opportunities. Such differences could indicate the extent of heads' powers over management systems, reflected the range of opportunities for micro-political bargaining in schools and indicated the influence of heads themselves over career processes.

Some of the career history heads had used the salary and promotion structure, and had responded to changes in their schools' situations, by producing substantially different systems of management. There were opportunities, despite the constraints, to alter management arrangements usually to counteract what were perceived by some heads to be difficulties inherent in hierarchical management arrangements. The opportunities for micro-political negotiation and for heads to exercise their political skills were extensive, as the following extracts will show.

Mr Stevens' account (p. 77) made reference to the two 'sides', the curriculum and the pastoral aspects, of management. For the majority of the career history heads these were two separate and distinct systems of management. However, some saw such a separation as a defect in terms of effective management of schools and also in terms of the career development of individual teachers. Some had engaged in micro-political activity to devise structures of management to prevent or to minimize such a divide. In the extracts which follow, the headteachers had identified the curriculum/pastoral divide as unhelpful for effective management in schools. This justification was an important part of their political strategy in their attempts to achieve change. In addition the heads were also concerned about the promotion difficulties some teachers could encounter as a result of following only one route. Such difficulties were likely to arise particularly for those teachers following the pastoral route. It seemed that a generally lower status was attached to pastoral responsibilities as compared with curriculum duties. In addition, there might also be gender differences in the career routes opted for. If women teachers tended to favour or to be encouraged into pastoral routes then women might, as a result, be more handicapped in the competition for senior management posts. Such equal opportunities arguments were likely to be effective in micro-political negotiations in schools, though clearly they would be more effective with some teachers and some groups of teachers than others. Heads would have to make strategic decisions in their choices of appropriate arguments and justifications for changes they wished to see made in the management arrangements in their schools.

Another aspect of hierarchical management that was perceived as a defect by some of the career history heads was the notion of hierarchy itself. In organizations such as schools which are staffed by professionals, a hierarchical structure of authority could be interpreted as inappropriate. Mrs Ince was particularly critical of the notion of hierarchical management in schools. The distribution of promotion posts in her school was designed to minimize the effects of hierarchy and thereby encourage the taking of initiatives by all the staff. She saw such arguments as the best way of justifying change in management structures. All the management positions in her school were affected. Hierarchy could not be eliminated, the salary and promotion structure prevented that. But the consequences could be ameliorated.

> We started off with three deputies, curriculum, pastoral and admin, and three senior teachers, somebody responsible for the lower school, someone for the upper school and somebody in charge of resources. But when I looked at the National Curriculum and LMS and so on, I decided we needed a change from that. We decided that we wanted lower, middle and upper school with a much more integrated pastoral/academic responsibility, to look at the curriculum in a horizontal way, possibly to become cost-centres under LMS.
>
> So I shall have two deputies and four senior teachers. We have made the heads of school, lower, middle and upper, pastoral *and* academic and it seemed that we would be going in for a repetitive exercise if we had a deputy head pastoral as well. Particularly since we quite genuinely believe that it is the tutor that matters pastorally, so all the rest of us are to empower the tutor; apart from that we have no role pastorally. I always think it is very, very important not to get into a position where somebody is given a responsibility and then someone else is put in a more senior position to monitor, because, well, that is one of the problems with management. We decided we would go for a varied set of responsibilities for each of the two deputies, with each having some curriculum responsibilities and some other responsibilities and sharing with me the responsibility for LMS.

We have only just started it this term so I don't really know if it is going to work out well, but that is what we decided to do.

Then we have course coordinators who are in charge of faculties. We deliberately went for the title course coordinators because we felt that there were so many points at which there was overlap. Broadly we have got Science; Communication (which is English and Modern Languages), Expressive Arts, Maths, Technology and Humanities.

Everybody is a tutor except the senior management team. We decided to go for a sort of mini-management team of E,D,B for each part of the school, lower, middle and upper. The holders of these allowances are responsible for overseeing and empowering tutors, enhancing tutors skills and particularly for curriculum awareness of what's going on and cross-curriculum things that are high profile in the National Curriculum.

I think it is a place which is very stimulating for teacher development in that you can really take on as much responsibility as you want to. As schools go it is less hierarchical than most and therefore if people want to do something they are able to do it.

(Mrs Ince; head of group 11 school)

This account demonstrates the extent of manoeuvring that headteachers could devise in their systems of management. The limits to change were set. The school had a fixed number or amount of promotional allowances, determined by its unit total. In addition, change was constrained by the inheritance of a particular management structure and others' expectations of what was an appropriate structure. Nevertheless the resulting system of management was significantly different from the examples so far demonstrated. Mrs Ince's justifications for change amounted to a political strategy that had worked in her school. The changes were under way. The modifications had affected all the management positions in the school. The deputies had varied responsibilities, each having some curriculum and some other whole-school tasks, while sharing the responsibility for LMS. There was a mini-management team for each of the three parts of the school and the allowances were designated primarily to empower the tutors who were the main pivot or fulcrum of the management system. In an attempt to ameliorate the impact of hierarchy, Mrs Ince's intention was for such a structure to stimulate teacher development, to spread responsibility and thereby to increase the taking of initiatives. Mrs Ince was very enthusiastic about these management arrangements and any difficulties (for example, of communication, of procedures, of overlapping and duplication of responsibilities) were not acknowledged, although the arrangements were new and not yet fully tested.

The next extract, from Mrs Cooper's account, demonstrated a different, though related, concern: the lower status of the pastoral. Mrs Cooper's account also showed similar justifications: the consequences for effective management and gender differences in the assignment of pastoral and curriculum responsibilities leading to promotion difficulties for women. Mrs Cooper's strategy was different to that of Mrs Ince, however. Mrs Cooper's micro-political negotiations had been concentrated on changing the responsibilities of those on lower incentive allowances and promotion positions.

> We've got a pastoral structure which is based on three sections
> with section leaders, year one and primary, years two, three and
> four, year five and out, with year teams of tutors underneath,
> and every single member of staff is attached in some way to a
> pastoral team. I put these teams first on purpose because they're
> often seen as secondary. Management of change has been mainly
> through the assistant team leaders and the tutors themselves. . . .
>   What are not conventional are the Cs and the Bs. The Cs
> are cross-curricula team leaders: Information Technology, TVEI,
> very general whole school briefs – coordinators we call them.
> The B posts are most unusual and I haven't come across
> anybody else who does this. It's really a legacy from my own
> experience when I had a joint [Head of Department and Head of
> House] role, because one so informed the other. Also, it was a
> move to try and get rid of single route promotion, either pastoral
> or academic, which usually operates against women. So at a B
> level we've got assistant team leaders who are both assistants to
> the pastoral section leaders and assistants to the curriculum
> team leaders. Now people say 'Oh this is too much for them'. But
> they are developmental roles and individuals can lead off from
> them into either sphere. It's quite precious to me because it's a
> real attempt to prevent people getting stuck in one promotion
> route or another.
>   (Mrs Cooper; head of what is now a group 10 school)

This account demonstrates how Mrs Cooper had had to adopt a different strategy in her attempt to change management. Micro-political negotiations had been focused on more junior staff. In the context of her school this represented a strategic decision and a political choice. She justified the need for change as a way of increasing the status of the pastoral and thereby making management more effective. Her assistant team leaders (B allowances) had both a pastoral and a curriculum brief.

In the final extract, Mrs Dexter's account also focuses on the need to change the pastoral/curriculum divide. Mrs Dexter similarly justified the change as necessary to make management more effective. However, Mrs Dexter's strategy was different from that of either Mrs Ince or Mrs Cooper; she had concentrated on senior management.

I've got three deputies at the moment but one is taking early retirement and we've decided not to replace the third deputy post, so from September we'll have one male and one female deputy. Then we've a senior tutor on an E allowance and she will oversee what I would call the school support systems and take a lead in care and guidance and she's also a year coordinator for the first year. Then I've got (seven) D allowance posts. Four are the other year coordinators who all have a whole-school responsibility as well as a year coordinator's job. That way they actually have a formalized access into the curriculum, into teaching styles and going into classrooms. I've worked in schools where the heads of year get all the complaints and they've absolutely no clout to go and deal with teachers whose teaching styles and approaches are causing the problems. So I was determined to avoid that. Each of the year coordinators has a responsibility, like records of achievement or community curriculum or post-16 continuity or TVEI coordination....

What we've tried to do is to give people experience. I think the difficulty is you have to create opportunities. I would hope that some of the year coordinator posts, which have a dual role of whole-school plus year coordinator, would actually operate as a stepping stone for people who may have been a head of department or a head of year and wanted a slightly broader experience before they went on to deputy headship.

(Mrs Dexter; head of a group 9 school)

Mrs Dexter's account justified the changes as necessary to ameliorate the effects of the pastoral/curriculum divide and to increase the status of the pastoral. She had developed her D allowance year coordinator posts to include a whole-school responsibility which gave them a formalized access into the cur-riculum. By such means she was able to increase the status of the pastoral and to provide a stepping stone for teachers in between head of department/head of year and deputy head positions. This strategy reflected her political judgment concerning the best way in her school of initiating change and making such changes acceptable to most of her staff.

The accounts of these three headteachers demonstrate both the extent and the limits to headteacher manoeuvrability in terms of their management systems. They had used their powers as senior managers/directors in order to modify and adapt the management systems in their schools. Their political skills or deficiencies were demonstrated in the different strategies they had adopted in order to promote change and to encourage its acceptance. The extent of their powers was considerable and their abilities to engage in micro-political negotia-tions were wide and various. They used perceived defects in the operation of hierarchical management structures in order to justify change. Any arguments against hierarchy and for collegiality could be very persuasive in schools where the notion of professionalism is often used to promote and support the idea of change. Such arguments were likely to be effective in convincing the large majority of teachers of the necessity of change. Other justifications used by the career history heads were the need to increase the status of pastoral responsibilities and the need to increase opportunities for women to enter senior management posts. Clearly it was a strategic decision by particular heads to use such arguments in their micro-political negotiations with staff. Not all staff would be convinced by such arguments, and indeed some teachers would object to them, particularly if their own interests were thereby threatened. Thus, whereas the idea of professionalism in teaching is a universally acknowledged and extensively supported justification for change, other justifications were likely to be more divisive and to increase differences and conflicts among school staffs. Headteachers could demonstrate their political acumen and skill in selecting appropriate reasons to justify change.

CONCLUSION

This chapter has attempted to illustrate the extent of secondary headteachers' powers to influence management systems, and the range of their abilities to influence promotion routes and career ladders, in their schools. The accounts given by the career history heads have been used to demonstrate both the limits to and the extent of their influence on the construction and development of management and career systems.

The national salary and promotion structure, and various educational changes, both constrain and give opportunities to heads to engage in micro-political activities in order to develop their systems of management. The allocation of promotion allowances to particular responsibilities is an important indication of a head's priorities and values. School structures of management are one of the ways in which heads can create their own schools. Heads are involved in micro-political negotiations with staff in order to implement what they see as desirable management arrangements. Any examination of organization theory, in respect of schools or any other organization, will need to include some analysis of the power of headteacher/managers and the political strategies used to influence, and maybe even to direct, the management systems in their school organizations. Headteachers' development of management systems and career and promotion structures in their schools are an important reflection of headship work culture and of what it means to be a headteacher.

It is important to emphasize that heads are only one of the participants in micro-political negotiations in schools. This chapter has focused on their powers and micro-political strategies, but other managers and classroom teachers have powers that they can use in their negotiations with heads. Headteachers, however, probably have more power resources than other micro-political actors in schools; their influence over the distribution of promotion positions is their greatest power resource, and British headteachers have a greater direct control over promotion than their counterparts in other countries (Hoyle, 1981). Their power to influence the distribution of promotion posts to particular tasks and duties makes them important definers and controllers of management. In addition, heads' provision of references for staff seeking promotion in other schools makes promotion a powerful resource of headteachers in their bargaining over tasks and responsibilities with teachers. In examining exchange theory and the 'goods' heads have to offer in return for getting jobs done and done well, Hoyle (1981) considered promotion to be very important in headteacher/teacher negotiations.

Some of the career history heads had worked hard using micro-political negotiations to devise and implement management systems that were unconventional. In this respect they could be termed pioneers or missionaries. It is not appropriate here to make any such assessment, one way or the other. Instead, the objective has been to emphasize the essentially political nature of heads' actions either to reproduce hierarchical management or to implement change. Both are political acts and a reflection of the extent of micro-political activities in school organizations.

The reproduction of hierarchical management is as political as the implementation of change. When headteachers say, as some might, that there is little they can do because the salary scale, or the need to combine posts because of falling rolls, necessitates such an outcome, then this justification is a strategic device. This paper has demonstrated that heads' powers can be extensive. Their political skills are obviously variable and their abilities to achieve consensus and avoid conflict will differ a great deal. However, the analysis of schools as micro-political organizations can clarify and extend our appreciation of how schools work as well as improve our understanding of what it means to be a headteacher.

It is also important to recognize that when headteachers, through micro-political negotiations, devise new management systems, they are through their actions affecting promotion ladders and career structures. Again, the interrelations between career actions and career structures should be stressed. In times of educational change, the abilities of actors (including headteachers) to modify career and promotion ladders are probably increased.

Chapter 7

Gender and Headship: Managerial Experiences

In teaching in schools women are concentrated in certain sectors and in general they predominate at the lower promotion levels. In Britain nearly all teachers and headteachers of nursery and separate infant schools are women. The majority of primary teachers (81 per cent in 1990) are women, yet 51 per cent of primary headteachers are men (DES, 1990). In secondary schools 48 per cent of teachers and 20 per cent of headteachers are women. In teaching women are marginalized less through numerical underrepresentation but more through ghetto-ization and concentration in women's enclaves such as class teaching in general and particularly teaching in nursery and infant schools. In teaching, as in all careers, women are underrepresented in senior positions which involve management tasks and which are achieved as a result of career promotions.

Women's underrepresentation in positions of management in schools has been well documented both in Britain (Acker, 1983, 1989; Ozga, 1992) and in the USA (Shakeshaft, 1987). However, in teaching some women do succeed in achieving career promotions into headship positions. Such women are an interesting group in terms of their coordination of career and gender identities. For the minority of women who do achieve secondary headships, they and their schools are more visible and likely to be subject to greater observation and scrutiny. Kanter (1977) claimed that where women are only a few, they get extra attention, are the subject of more gossip, stories and rumours, and are always in the spotlight. Ball (1987) described the additional pressures on women who are highly visible as a result of their minority position. Acker (1980) explained a fear of visibility, which has prompted some women to play down, hide and minimize traits or behaviours that might be seen as feminine and therefore as inappropriate in a managerial role. Using the career history material it was possible to examine in a preliminary way gender differences in headship styles and in management strategies. It was also possible to begin to explore the range of experiences of career and gender identity for women headteachers.

Career and gender can be experienced as problematic if the managerial responsibilities of headship are perceived as being at odds or in conflict with gender identity. Cultural contradictions have been perceived as inherent in career and management positions for women (Kanter, 1977; Chapman, 1978; Marshall, 1984). Women who enter the world of career and promotion into management are taking part in social relationships determined by masculine values. Career, promotion and management as presently constituted are areas where the values of scientific rationality, bureaucratic objectivity and hierarchical authority can be at odds with the caring, subjective, relational values which are supposedly important to women. It is possible that promotion-successful women will become absorbed by the managerialist values and structures which they have had to learn to operationalize in order to succeed. We have to ask, therefore, what happens to women who do manage, who have built careers and achieved promotions?

The answer to this question is important. It is intended to explore this in a preliminary way by considering the experiences of the women headteachers in the career history group. Can women headteachers operationalize a different style of headship? Are their schools different kinds of social organizations? Can gender liberate and transform headship or does the headteacher role neutralize gender identity? Are there gender differences in managerial leadership styles and in the experience of being a headteacher?

LEADERSHIP STYLES: GENDER DIFFERENCES

When researchers have focused their attentions on gender differences in management, then the question of leadership 'style' becomes the point at issue. Gender differences in terms of the definitions of objectives, perceptions of the organization and task completion, are not significant, but in terms of manner of execution of tasks and style of leadership, then gender becomes an important differentiating variable. The concept leadership *style* needs some preliminary explanation. Ball (1987, p. 83) gave the following definition:

> A style is a form of social accomplishment, a particular way of
> realizing and enacting the authority of headship. It is eminently
> an individual accomplishment, but at the same time it is
> essentially a form of joint action.

In his analysis of the micro-politics of schools Ball expressed the organizational task of the head (1987, p. 82) as the need to achieve and maintain control (the problem of domination), while encouraging and ensuring social order and commitment (the problem of integration). Heads manage their schools in different ways according to Ball: some rely on their own leadership qualities; others emphasize their bureaucratic responsibilities. Some heads manage by means of personal influence and conviction; some through authority and control; while others manage through committee structures and hierarchies of delegation. Heads give indications to others, to staff, pupils, parents, advisers, governors, as to their preferred or intended style by means of verbal, non-verbal and written communications, in face-to-face encounters, informal and formal meetings. When the leadership/management style is acceptable, then joint action can proceed. When the style is unacceptable, however, then relationships become strained and conflict might develop.

The difficulties of demonstrating gender differences in leadership style have been discussed by Shakeshaft (1987). She argued that there might be substantial contrasts and contradictory findings between studies which used observation and work diaries compared with the findings of studies which used specially devised questionnaires involving measurement of leadership perceptions. Her own analysis (Shakeshaft, 1979, 1985), using a Leadership Behaviour Description Questionnaire, found no differences between males and females on twelve dimensions of leadership behaviour: representation, demand reconciliation, tolerance of uncertainty, persuasiveness, initiation of structure, tolerance of freedom, role assumption, consideration, production emphasis, predictive accuracy, integration and superior orientation. However, other researchers using research techniques such as observation *have* found gender differences.

Most of the research into gender differences in leadership styles has been American. Such research has been fairly small-scale, however, and relatively inconclusive. Adkison (1981) suggested that female compared with male principals were more likely to involve themselves in instructional supervision, to exhibit a democratic leadership style and to concern themselves with students. Such differences were confirmed by Shakeshaft's analysis of the head as educational leader and master teacher compared with the head as manager and administrator. Cochran (1980) noted that women principals were more effective at resolving conflicts, at motivating teachers, and at acting as representatives rather than directors of a group.

The question of leadership style and of gender differences is difficult to handle empirically. The results of quantitative testing procedures designed to be used on large samples have found few significant differences between male and female heads in their perceptions of leadership or their rankings of the task performances of headship. However, qualitative studies, usually small-scale, but considerably more detailed, *have* suggested gender differences in style. The question of 'leadership style' is difficult for researchers to take over and to operationally define. A style of leadership is a manner of working, an approach, a feeling, a method and a way and as such it is elusive and intangible, problematic to measure and to demonstrate.

There are difficulties, therefore, in demonstrating gender differences in management and leadership style. For a number of years, researchers argued that there were no significant differences. Shakeshaft (1987) claimed that it was not difficult to demonstrate ways in which men and women did the same things when they managed. The women would not have been selected for management unless they could complete the tasks and comprehend and master the managerial culture. Shakeshaft also argued that to claim no difference had been a political strategy used by both supporters and opponents of the need to encourage more women into senior positions. For women's advocates the 'no differences' argument enabled them to refute notions that women would be less effective than men as managers. For opponents, it was politically desirable to report no differences since it was then possible to explain the small numbers of women in educational management by reference to the lack of demand from larger numbers of women in that they refused to apply and put themselves forward for such positions.

The lack of success of such arguments, in terms of increasing the proportions of women in educational leadership posts, led Shakeshaft (1987) to take up a different position. She argued that there *are* differences and that in certain organizations, like schools, feminine styles of leadership and management are more appropriate and effective. Similarly Gray (1987, p. 299) claimed that if schools as organizations 'are perceived as needing to be caring, nurturing, maintaining, supporting, understanding, they will be seen to require a form of management that for many is essentially a stereotype of femininity'. While warning against stereotyping by gender, Gray argued that management needs to draw on 'intuition, calculated risk taking, aesthetic considerations, dependence on colleagues, messiness and incompleteness'. These were for Gray the 'feminine' aspects of all personalities since in terms of stereotypes he claimed ' "real" men do not make mistakes!'.

In Britain, there have been several attempts to describe the leadership styles of headteachers (Lyons, 1974; Peters, 1976; Earley and Weindling, 1987). Qualitative researchers have provided useful insights into the way a headship style is negotiated (Burgess, 1983, 1984; Ball, 1987; Gillborn, 1989). Few, however, have alluded to *gender* differences in leadership style. Indeed, significant differences have usually been denied (Earley and Weindling, 1987; Hall, Mackay and Morgan, 1986). So what happens to the women who do achieve promotion to the senior management positions of secondary headship?

The analysis of the responses from the career history headteachers demonstrated a great deal of variation both amongst the women and amongst the men. There were differences in leadership and management styles but few of the differences were clearly gender-related. It is important to note that some of the male heads emphasized collegial relations and participatory forms of management in schools while some of the female heads were inclined towards hierarchy and authority in management. Significant differences in styles of leadership are not difficult to demonstrate in general (see Chapter 6), although the clear linkage of style with gender is more problematic. Ball (1987) analysed four ideal-type categories of leadership style (interpersonal, managerial, political-adversarial and political-authoritarian) and in his subsequent elaboration and illustration of these styles, he does not mention gender differences. Perhaps we should conclude from such an omission that gender was not a significant variable in differentiating these types.

What is significant, however, is an emphasis on style rather than on gender. Stereotypes of masculinity and femininity are not helpful except in so far as they better enable us to assess what are the best qualities and styles in any individual, whether man or woman (Archer and Lloyd, 1982). Similarly with managerial and leadership styles, the objective in demonstrating differences is not to enable us to claim that either women or men make the best headteachers. However, where differences are demonstrated we are then in a better position to ask which, in that time and at that place, is the best style of management and leadership in the organization that is the school. The most important criterion of good management is that it should relate to the organizational needs of the institution. Such needs are both structural (continuity and replacement) and cultural (including working relations and practices). In the case of headship of secondary schools, therefore, we need to ask which aspects of managerial and leadership style best suit the needs of schools in the current economic and political climate. This is a much more intriguing and relevant question. Our answers in terms of most appropriate style will vary from school to school and area to area. Opinions will differ and may even conflict. In addition, circumstances will alter as external conditions change the needs of the organization that is the school.

EXPERIENCING HEADSHIP: GENDER DIFFERENCES

If it is difficult to demonstrate conclusively that there are consistent gender differences in styles of headship, it is not difficult to show gender differences in the *experience* of headship. Analysis of the experiences of the holders of particular occupational positions and the effects of work roles on worker identities has been an important contribution of interactionist research. Such a viewpoint concentrates on how people construct meanings and understandings in everyday relations and activities at work. Woods (1983) explained such an approach in respect of teachers (and pupils) in schools and the study by Lortie (1975) of the American schoolteacher is regarded as a classic analysis of teacher experiences. In considering the experience of headship, it is important to consider the process of *becoming* a headteacher and the everyday experiences involved in *being* a head. In respect of both of these, there are significant gender differences.

Becoming a Headteacher

The process of becoming a headteacher is one of adult socialization into a managerial identity. It involves assuming the tasks and responsibilities of headship and developing a management style which is worked at and realized in each encounter (Goffman, 1971; Ball, 1987). There has been little research on becoming a *head*teacher although there have been a number of studies of *teacher* socialization which have concentrated on the early years in teaching (Hanson and Herrington, 1976; Taylor and Dale, 1971; Lacey, 1977). Lacey elaborated a model of teacher socialization using the notion of strategy in order to emphasize the teacher's own impact and input into the process of assuming a teacher identity. Nias (1984) used the concept of self in order to examine the definition and maintenance of self in primary teaching.

In the process of becoming a headteacher most heads will have been well prepared for their headship tasks and responsibilities as a result of a succession of career moves and promotions. The various positions on the promotion ladder of the teaching career prepare them for the duties of headship and their experience of different schools makes them aware of the differences in style of leadership of particular headteachers. The perceptions of career through individualistic success in competition for promotion posts and the increased responsibility and authority acquired through successive promotion achievements are common to all heads experiences.

Gender differences in experience are likely to become more obvious as the higher levels of promotion ladders are reached, however. Although the competition for headship is severe for every applicant since there are few posts available, it is likely to be experienced as more severe by women because they feel at a disadvantage. In the career history group of headteachers, Miss Hollis explained the difficulties she had in achieving a headship post (see pp. 42–3). Although she met the criteria of merit, achievement, wide experience and an ability to manage and lead, she felt there were additional problems for her because she was a woman. Many men are also unsuccessful in the competition for headship posts but for them gender is not a factor in their failure. Several of the heads reported the widely held view that the appointment of a woman head by selection panels was regarded as more of a risk. The lay members of selection panels, parent governors in particular, would advise caution and conservatism in headteacher appointments. In this way gender could override other merit-determined criteria in selectors' decisions. Anti-discrimination legislation would be little help since appointment decisions could always be couched in terms of merit and explained as gender-neutral.

Being a Head

The experience of headship refers to the everyday activities involved in *being* a headteacher. Such experiences also vary according to gender. For men headteachers there are likely to be few problems arising from gender identity. A headmaster's *style* might result in conflict in school if it does not meet the expectations of staff, pupils and parents. But for men the conflict arises from style and not from gender. Similarly some women headteachers experience few difficulties associated with their gender. In the career history group, Mrs Grainger explained how, for her, gender was unproblematic in her achievement of a headteacher identity.

> I am very much *not* a feminist except that I totally believe in
> female equality. It's an issue sometimes that I discuss with the

women on my staff because there are women on my staff who
care about being called 'chairperson' or get twitchy if they see a
letter addressed to 'the headmaster'. They mind that we still
have about a million report forms that we'll be using up to the
year dot that say 'headmaster' on the bottom and (they) would
prefer that I just threw them all in the bin and wasted them all.

I care not one jot for any of that. I think it utterly boring. I
work in a sphere where every time there is a meeting of the
headteachers, secondary heads in Pennington, there are only
seven female secondary heads and eighty-one men. And of course
I've arrived late at a meeting sometimes and been walking along
a row looking for an empty space and one of them will say 'Sit
here, if you like Joan' (patting knee) and I'll say 'Well, you might
like it for ten minutes but you wouldn't like it for longer than
that' or 'I'll find a better lap than yours' or something. 'Cause I
think it's funny, I actually think it's quite a compliment. I'd start
to worry if I didn't get remarks like that because as a female I
like clothes, I like perfume, I like jewellery, I like men. Apart
from that I live my life as if I were a man. And it doesn't occur
to me not to; it doesn't occur to me that it's a problem. But I
don't know why it doesn't and I would dearly love to know why
it doesn't because I'd like to instil that in the girls here in school.

(Mrs Grainger)

In this extract, the headteacher perceived no difficulties in reconciling her
gender and headship identities. Her gender was important to her sense of self
and well-being but it was not perceived as problematic in the way she wished to
run her school.

For other women heads, however, gender did intrude in their experiences of
headship. Mrs Cooper had kept a log of sexist comments, harassment and
embarrassment which she had experienced. These experiences were not confined
to school but also intruded at heads' and local education authority meetings, at
social gatherings, and professional association conferences.

At my first meeting with other heads in the Authority I was
conspicuous as one of only eight women heads in a force of
seventy-eight and was asked by a male head, 'Do you know why
they appointed a *woman* at [your school]?' He had no idea that
this was offensive. An adviser thought that the LEA now had 'a
lot of women heads'. In school in another context a fairly senior
colleague said, 'Presumably you were appointed for your ideas.' I
quickly got used to being welcomed as the *wife* of a head at
heads' meetings and to comments on my clothes and looks.
During a lunch-time off-the-record discussion a woman deputy
head known to me was discussed. The reason for her

non-appointment to headship was advanced: her dress was too flamboyant and she wore heavy make-up and jewellery! Typically I was asked one evening (by the male chair of governors) whether I was going to change my clothes. I was wearing casual trousers and a sweatshirt-type top for a community association meeting.

I got used to being accused openly of being 'too soft' when dealing with difficult pupils because I listened to them and did not usually raise my voice. A male head of year followed such a comment with the remark that of course I knew more about girls then he did.

On the telephone I frequently met disbelief when I clarified my identity after a query. I was usually taken for a secretary; after clearly stating that I was the head I was asked 'the head of which department?' on one occasion. Face to face, a computing salesman used my first name without asking, while the superintendent of parks and gardens greeted me with 'Hello, young lady'! and the caretaking supervisor risked 'You are gorgeous'!

(Mrs Cooper)

For this woman head, gender was intrusive and prominent in her experience of headship. Similar experiences were related by others amongst the women heads and were felt by some to interfere in managerial relationships in schools. Mrs Ince had taken steps to try to ameliorate some of the difficulties which she felt women experienced in managerial arrangements in schools.

I have come to see how weighted the scales are against women in management in that almost all my dealings are with men. Almost all the officers I deal with are men; a large number of my senior colleagues at school are men and most of my fellow heads are men. I think that I have only allowed myself to really become aware of that as I have become more confident in being a head and when just occasionally I found myself interviewing with only women on the panel. It suddenly occurred to me what a different experience that is and that men have that experience practically all the time.

I have recently felt able to make a very deliberate effort to encourage women in the school to look at themselves as potential managers. We have talked a lot about our difficulties, about our strengths and the fact that the whole business of competitive interview actually suits men a great deal better than women. A lot of business is decided at meetings and that meetings, on the whole, suit men, large formal meetings particularly.

(Mrs Ince)

It seemed, then, that for the women heads in the career history groups gender was a part of their experience of headship and for some of these women gender was intrusive in managerial relations in schools and in perceptions of headship identity. For men heads their gender is positively associated with increased managerial responsibility and authority in their schools, but for women heads it can be intrusive in managerial arrangements and a constant threat to the authority of headship. Gender can intrude in the process of becoming a headteacher, if women feel there might be discrimination in selection processes. And gender can intrude in the experience of being a head, if the women's minority status results in difficulties in managing staff, children and parents as well as in dealings with school governors, local education authority officials and other personnel.

CONCLUSION

This chapter has examined firstly the question of gender differences in style of headship of secondary schools and secondly the different ways in which gender and headship can be experienced. Research evidence has confirmed significant differences in headship style but the association of such style differences with gender is less conclusive. It is important in this connection to remember the comments of Scott (1986) concerning the ahistorical nature of arguments which attempt to assert that the differences between men and women are universal and unchanging. It is more appropriate and indeed optimistic to assume that notions of masculinity and femininity are historically and societally specific and hence are able to change and be changed. If style rather than gender is the critical variable, then we are in a better position to be able to determine which, at any particular time and any particular place, is the best style of management in the organization that is the school.

In respect of the experiences of men and women headteachers, this chapter has explored some of the different ways in which the career history group of headteachers experienced gender and headship. For the men headteachers, gender was unproblematic in negotiating a headship and leadership style. For some women heads gender was likewise unproblematic. For others of the women heads, however, gender was intrusive both in becoming a head and in the experience of headship.

The cultural power of sex role stereotyping needs to be acknowledged for this is the source of the managerial conflicts experienced by some women headteachers. There is increasing awareness that stereotypes reflect a group's work roles and the kind of activities in which we see them engaged (Eagly, 1987). Thus sex role stereotypes arise in response to the sexual division of labour and occupational segregation in home and workplace. When women are absent from senior management positions or only a minority of women hold such posts, as in the headship of secondary schools, then women are not characterized in terms of their authority and leadership abilities but rather in terms of their identities as *women* headteachers. Furthermore, sex role stereotyping causes us to make the mistake of attributing occupational segregation to personality differences. Thus we assume that the nurturant and submissive behaviour of (female) secretaries results from women's personality characteristics, not the role requirements imposed by the work situation (O'Leary and Ickovics, 1992). These gender stereotypes, deriving from the sexual division of labour, come to constitute normative beliefs to which people tend to conform or are induced to conform. This is the cultural power and force of sex role stereotyping which results in the double-bind for women in management positions in schools and elsewhere.

There is clear evidence that headteachers manage in diverse ways, have a wide variety of personality traits and leadership styles and skills. There are differences in style between headteachers but few of these differences are consistently gender-related. It seems also that gender differences in the experience of headship, some of which have been illustrated, stem primarily from women's minority status. For the minority of women who do achieve secondary headships, they and their schools are more visible and likely to be subject to greater observation and scrutiny. The women heads in the career history study frequently referred to the double-edged aspect of being more visible. At least they and their schools were noticed and remembered; the women's 'deviant' gender status ensured such recognition. At the same time, these women felt that they were constantly on trial; as representatives of their gender they were fearful to put a foot wrong since their mistakes would be used to condemn all women headteachers (although similar mistakes by men are not used to argue the unsuitability of men for headship). Such pressures were acute and constant. The additional pressures on women who are highly visible as a result of their minority position have been discussed by a number of researchers (Kanter, 1977; Acker, 1980; Ball, 1987).

Some of the women heads in the career history group were troubled by the intrusion of gender into their professional work relationships and responsibilities. Only the promotion of more women into senior management positions in schools (and elsewhere) will shatter the stereotypical conceptions of men as managers and women as assistants. O'Leary and Ickovics (1992) have suggested, following Eagly (1987), that the way to minimize the power of sex-stereotyping is to emphasize the *other* identity, such as headteacher or manager. By removing the gender link we might eventually be able to avoid the cultural stereotyping deriving from the sexual division of labour. The critical issue will then become headteacher management style and how appropriate styles can be operationalized by both men and women headteachers. In terms of career, the headteacher management style is a critical part of the career structure and process which facilitates or impedes teachers in taking appropriate career action.

Chapter 8

Career Concerns: When Promotion Ladders Seem to End

The headteacher position in England is currently the peak, the top management post in schools. But what happens to those who do achieve such headteacher posts? Do their promotions continue or is the headship the final career position? Ambitious men teachers can achieve headships when they are in their thirties (Hilsum and Start, 1974) although the median age for women is probably in their forties. So having reached a career peak, how do individual men and women heads view the remainder of their careers? For some, this will amount to another twenty-five to thirty years of their professional working lives.

When Smith (1975) examined the career structure of headteachers in a Midlands city, he found considerable movement of heads between posts. He did add, however, 'that this was a period when many schools were reorganized and a third of the moves were a direct consequence of these changes' (Smith, 1975, p. 34). Other research projects (e.g. Earley and Weindling, 1988) would seem to indicate substantial career stability among headteachers once in post. It is also important to emphasize that movement between headteacher posts, even if it occurs, might only be perceived as a sideways move and does not necessarily constitute promotion and career progress for heads.

In order to understand the career implications of reaching the headteacher position, it is necessary to return once again to consider the meaning of career and consider what are the consequences, for headteachers themselves, their professional associations and their employers of reaching the top of the teaching career ladder.

Over the past thirty years or so, there has been a tremendous increase in the development and elaboration of career structures within organizations and professions. This has been connected with the regularization of salaries and the need to offer formal and standardized career opportunities usually to male non-manual workers. In teaching the national career structure is defined in terms of basic salary scale and has incentive allowances, senior, head of department, deputy and headship positions as staging posts in the career. Years of teaching service determine position on the salary scale, but different responsibilities (usually administrative and managerial) mark promotion on the career ladder.

In Chapter 2 the two frames of reference, career action and career structure, were illustrated and it was argued that both are inseparable and essential in any analysis of career. The linking of actions and structures and the formation of career structures out of individuals' actions also has important implications for headteachers' careers. In a time of rapid educational change, headteachers and their professional associations need to be aware of the link between career actions and career structures. Current changes, such as LMS and the possible demise of the LEAs, might open up further career prospects for headteachers. Also, where wider changes affect the demand for particular professional practitioners (such as educational advisers and inspectors as well as educational finance and business consultants) and, as a result, change the rules defining who gets particular positions, then career patterns might be altered. In this way career structures might be changed as well as career expectations.

CAREER SATISFACTION

It was the accounts of the career history headteachers which alerted me to the significance of the experience of reaching the top in career terms; of concerns about what happens when the top levels of promotion ladders are achieved. Not all the heads expressed concern about their careers. Both age and gender were significant in explaining the differences between heads in terms of these anxieties. Concern about their futures was predominantly expressed by male heads in their forties and early fifties. For the most part, further career development was not a worry for the newly in post or older heads or for women. Headteachers who expressed little or no concern could be grouped into four categories. The first category included those headteachers who were fairly new to their posts. For those who had been in their headships for less than five or six years, the interest, challenge and stimulus of the job, particularly in a time of rapid and extensive change, was sufficient. They were enjoying their newly achieved status and appreciating the benefits as well as the responsibilities of the job. They were still learning how to operationalize their objectives and how to mediate and negotiate with their staff. The job was a challenge; there was still a lot to be done. Both men and women heads were in this category and the years in post ranged from one year to six.

The second category included those heads who were anticipating retirement either through age or ill-health. For these heads the time for concern about career was past. Both men and women heads were in this category and Miss Reeves' account of coming to terms with the end of career development was representative of such heads' experiences:

> I have thought of leaving once or twice but it was a bit late
> really to get anything else. I mean I wouldn't have left in less
> than five years but by the time five years was over I'd made a
> lot of friends here and I was over 50. So that was the end of that
> really. Whatever I applied for I don't think they even took up
> the references as far as I know.

But maybe I wasn't quite so keen as I had been earlier to
move. I don't know. There were various sorts of peripheral
things (such as) the school centenary and I really should have
been looking around a bit before that but I thought I can't leave
in the year of the centenary. I'd a friend who was ill and she died
and I couldn't leave in the middle of that. Things like that, but
nothing that need have stopped me I think if I'd just been a bit
younger.

(Miss Reeves; age 56; a head for eleven years)

The third category included those headteachers who had been in their present positions for approximately ten years but who were content to remain.
Career progress for these heads was to continue in their posts because a job was
still to be done. Their current headships remained interesting and challenging.
Heads in this category often demonstrated a charismatic zeal and enthusiasm
for their jobs which was labelled the style of the 'autocratic pastoral missioner'
by Hughes (1972). Career promotion had ended but career development continued. Both men and women heads were in this category, as the accounts of Mr
Johnson and Mrs Ince illustrated:

This is my eleventh year which is an extraordinary long time.
But I still feel an immense sense of freshness. Not all the time,
but this is the kind of school, I believe, in which the sort of
ideals and ambitions and aims that I have for education can be
reached for. In Browning's terms, can be reached for and can be
touched, if not wholly grasped. It is because of that, that there is
a challenge here. There is a challenge everywhere in education,
but there is a challenge here which you can feel, I feel can be
excitingly met. Because of that, I see no reason, I have no desire
at the moment to leave.

(Mr Johnson; age 47; a head for eleven years)

This is such a difficult school to leave and I have no interest in
applying for a bigger school. I do not know why. But being head
of this school is a very, very different experience from being
head of most schools, a much more pleasant one. I think I would
find it really hard to cope with a different school in the sense
that I think it is quite exceptional in terms of commitment of
teachers and their enthusiasm for what they are doing ... I just
think that I have had a very different experience of being a head
from most people.

(Mrs Ince; age 56; a head for nine years)

The fourth category also included heads who were content to remain in their
present posts, who were not concerned about further movement or additional

promotion. But for these heads their careers in teaching, their occupational successes and achievements, were counterbalanced by other roles, by different sorts of responsibilities and interests both inside education and outside it. In this category there were male and female heads but there were gender differences. Thus although the men and women heads might have additional educational interests and concerns (active participation in professional associations and trade unions, and responsibilities for training), it was really only the women heads who balanced their careers as headteachers with different aspects of themselves, for example with their family and other roles. In terms of explaining their lack of career concern, such women were able to experience satisfaction with their career *and* other achievements. This prevented and avoided any anxiety about further career progress. The accounts of Mrs Grainger and Mrs Morley illustrated the balancing of careers achieved by some of the women heads:

> I wonder very much what I want to do next. In fact this last weekend I have been toying with whether or not I want to do a year's secondment to go and work on the LMS package at County Hall. In the event I'm not going to do that. It is fairly chaotic at County Hall at the moment. I do actually work a great deal out of school as well as in the school for education in that I'm convenor for the SHA in Penns County and I also serve on the executive of [a county professional association of headteachers]. And I'm part of an Inset working team who have as their brief to provide in-service training for Penns' headteachers.
>
> And that more or less brings me to where we are except that my unpaid career is as important to me as my paid career. I started off at university as choreographer to the Operatic Society and discovered that I actually sang better than most of their singers. In the arrogant way of youth, at the age of 19, I produced, choreographed and starred in *The Beggar's Opera*. I've been singing in and directing opera ever since, mostly on a freelance basis, mostly amateur though I've done professional things for the radio. And for the last three years my husband and I have run our own theatre company. People always say how do you manage to do both things, and I think the only answer is that I don't know what it's like not to do both things because I've done them both for such a long time.
>
> Occasionally I've seen a job in the education world that sounds interesting and that's been somewhere different geographically. But the fact that [my opera work] has taken quite an exciting turn of events recently means that physically I have to be near the theatre I have a contact with. But that's only transient, it's not a major problem. I also do believe that if

I wanted the new job most, then I would go for it anyway. The fact that I don't suggests that it isn't top of my order of priorities.

(Mrs Grainger; age 49; a head for seven years)

I was never caught up in the urge for promotion like some teachers seem to be. Maybe it's because I was happily married and have a very positive life outside school.

Our main involvement is in the United Reform Church. My husband is a non-stipendiary minister and I'm an elder in the church, so really that has been an important part of our life. There was a lot of youth work connected with that in the past, including representing the church nationally. I went to America to represent them, to youth camps; I've worked on national committees and governing bodies within the church set-up.

And my family has been very important in my career. I think my family has been crucial. I couldn't have done what I have done and got where I have got or had the satisfaction I've had, without the support of various people like mother, mother-in-law, husband, father. It's not dragged me down or made for difficulties and you can't say that about everybody in teaching.

(Mrs Morley; age 58; a head for five years)

In the group of career history headteachers, the newly appointed and the older heads, those who retained a missionary-type educational zeal and enthusiasm, and those, predominantly women, with other interests and affiliations, had not experienced concerns about their careers. For other heads, however, particularly those who had achieved their headships young, had been in post for more than five years, who were now in mid-career and who were male, their career concerns were important and influential in their experiences of headship.

CAREER CONCERNS

I would have thought that you would ask about the fact that I am 50, I've been here nine years and I don't have to retire until I am 65. 1 suppose everybody who gets to 50 feels the same; that they are too old for the market place to consider them to be interesting propositions but not old enough to consider themselves past it. So they're locked into the consequences of a decision they made several years ago. I feel I am locked into a move I made when I was 41 and obviously a saleable

commodity. But now I am 50 and I don't think I can make
another headship move; I don't think governors look at
50-year-olds.

So what do you do? Do I hack it out here? I mean every day
is different, every year is different, there is a lot of development
going on. I enjoy the school day, but isn't there something else I
could do? I can't answer that question. You see I have been a
headteacher for half of my working life. There should be
something else I could move to. One or two heads become
inspectors/advisers. But I mean I couldn't advise on subjects. I
could advise headteachers and I do occasionally, informally, but
how long would I be a good adviser of headteachers with the
current rate of change?

(Mr Lane; age 50; a head for fourteen years; current headship
nine years)

This head's account reflected the career concerns of a number of the mid-
career male headteachers. To the extent that the minority of women who become
heads, achieve their headships later and also often have second careers in addition, career concerns would be less problematic. The women in the career history
study had not voiced such concerns. The problem for the men heads seemed to
arise because of the termination of the obvious career ladder and these heads'
early achievement of the top promotion post. Most of these heads recognized
that they would probably continue in their present positions for the remainder
of their working careers. But although the likelihood of this was high, it was
regarded as a very unsatisfactory situation and certainly no solution to their
career concerns. A secondment might bring a short span of temporary relief but
would not resolve the career dilemma.

Since becoming a head I've found there's just too much to do in
the job itself and as a head I've become very much a sort of
school-based head. And I now regret it because after twenty
years in education there's nothing I would like more than for
somebody to offer me an opportunity to become refreshed.

I'm feeling it. It may not be apparent this morning, the sun's
shining, but I really do feel it. I've gone one hundred per cent for
being here, for heading things. I mean we were the first school in
Mertonshire to issue records of achievement. We really set
ourselves up as the leading school and I played a leading role in
it. And alright I've visited many schools and I've run courses
and I've had lots of people in. I mean that's satisfying and I
suppose you could say that takes me beyond the confines of the
school.

But I would like something that took me out of school and
broadened me and gave me something else to think about apart

from just school. I've still got twenty years in me. Give me a
year's secondment.

> (Mr Stevens; age 44; a head for six years)

Mr Stevens was one of the younger heads still relatively new in post. In certain respects his style of headship illustrated the charismatic missionary zeal enthusiasm already discussed as a factor which could allay career concern. Yet anxiety about his career and about maintaining his initial enthusiasm and freshness were beginning to be experienced. As he himself explained, Mr Stevens had to try to sustain the challenge of headship for another twenty years.

In considering their own situations, some of the heads had tried to make recommendations and devise solutions to their career concerns. Most of their suggestions were modest and consisted of a career structure for headteachers in which headships were achieved first in smaller schools and then promotion and movement to larger schools would constitute additional steps on the career ladder. Such a career structure for heads was already a possibility, of course, although the policy of LEAs towards the movement of headteachers was a critical factor. According to the career history heads, the two Midlands authorities in this research had different attitudes, if not different policies, in respect of the movement of heads. Excluding reorganization, which had affected heads in one county, only two of the twenty headteachers (one man in each county) had had two headships.

> I am not aware that LEAs are reluctant to move heads and I do
> know of several heads in Mertonshire who have worked in more
> than one Mertonshire school.
>
> I have wondered whether I might have been wiser staying
> where I was and persisting with applications for headships of
> smaller schools because I was concerned that I got to the top
> rather quickly and it looks as though I could end up in this
> school for nearly twenty-five years.
>
> There is a career structure for heads if you start with a
> smaller school. You can work your way through larger ones. You
> can start at a group nine or group ten and then work your way
> up to a group twelve.
>
> > (Mr Hall; age 53; a head for sixteen years)

> In Penns County, I think there is a policy not to move heads. It
> appears that there is very little prospect of heads having a
> career as a head. I have been very fortunate in that I have been
> head of two schools which I think were different, which gave me
> a new lease of life and new challenges; this one was a very big
> challenge.
>
> I would recommend some sort of career structure for heads
> in terms of, if you like, trying them out in little schools and if

they succeed they should be promoted to a bigger school with more responsibility. . . .

I mean why don't they give opportunities for some highly successful heads of smaller schools to increase their expertise and experience in a larger school on a firm foundation in a smaller school. I don't know but it would seem logical to me because it would be a sort of promotion. But it does not seem to work that way. I can only think of three heads that have moved and sometimes when a head is appointed as a young man they get stale after ten years.

(Mr Draper; age 59; a head for twenty years; current headship nine years)

One headteacher was more wide-ranging in his interpretation of the problem and more radical in his perception of a solution. The singularity and locked-in nature of career routes when once embarked upon, was seen by him to be the major problem for headteachers. More flexibility and more transferability of skills between and across educational sectors was perceived as a potential solution. More career moves and career developments that were horizontal rather than just vertical within schools would be essential if structures were to be opened up and wider access encouraged.

I achieved a headship at the age of thirty-six, so in a sense the Authority had the problem of having promoted in a young head; and what happens when the young head becomes the older head and so on. I think I've stayed too long in one post and at the age of fifty-three I certainly am not going anywhere in promotional terms I wouldn't think.

One of the features of the education service is although it's an education service covering polytechnics, universities, county halls, administration, inspectorship, advisership, HMIs, tertiary colleges, schools, whatever, yet as a global education service there is no unity in it. Once you take one particular track in one particular aspect of the service you tend to be rigidly held to that track. I think transferability has been absent. If you wanted promotion in administration at County Hall then you went through that route and so on and so on. My suspicion is that in the last three or four years the pattern has changed: more heads *are* going from headships to become Chief Education Officers. People who have gone through the administrative route at County Hall are suddenly finding that their promotion prospects are affected by people coming in from schools. So maybe there is more flexibility.

But I still can't see it. I mean I have no hope of using my experience of seventeen years headship and moving to a university department. They couldn't afford me anyway. Or of my becoming a director of a polytechnic or easily becoming a principal of a further education college.

Yet if you look at the whole range of management experience you get in one sector, those skills must be transferable. If we are teaching transferable skills to youngsters and we have supposedly got them ourselves, then that isn't reflected in the opportunities of career progression or transfers of career.

Careers in education have been too locked in and there ought to be national mechanisms of training that allow cross-fertilization between sectors; and promotion in and out of the various sectors, either through a more vigorous or better applied secondment policy by LEAs (of course that's going up the creek as well as with LMS) or simply by wider involvement of partners in education. That has not been a strong feature of the British educational scene. I have worked with the university on training deputy heads and doing some management training, and that's been great. But the amount of time I have been able to spend in other sectors of education is almost nil and that's not right. The skills ought to be transferable across various sectors of education but the mechanisms and salary scales don't allow for that.

(Mr Bennett; age 53; a head for seventeen years)

In Mr Bennett's account, the career structures, the promotion ladders and the salary scales in teaching had operated to confine careers within narrow routes and tracks. There was little or no flexibility and no transferability of skills and expertise. As a consequence, when the promotion ladder for teachers had been climbed and when the top rung, the headteacher position, had been scaled, then there was little opportunity for promotion-successful individuals to further develop their careers. Having absorbed, accepted, used and succeeded in the traditional career requirements, having mastered the skills that had resulted in regular movement and steady promotion, the careers of such heads came to a sudden and unanticipated stop. In their experience there was nowhere else to go.

CONCLUSION

The career concerns of these headteachers indicated that this might constitute a problem of importance for the profession and one which has important policy and manpower planning implications for those who are the employers of teachers (whether local or central government in England). The career history research can give no estimation of size or extent of career concern although this chapter has indicated which heads were likely to be affected and which heads were likely to be able to avoid such concerns.

The understandings and experiences of career of teachers and, in this case, headteachers reinforce and reproduce a model of career that is normal. Individuals *expect* careers that develop, through vertical promotion levels where each additional level has increased responsibilities, different (usually managerial and administrative) functions, wider powers, and higher salaries and status. Promotion and progress are perceived as necessary characteristics of a developing career. When experiences confirm expectations, then career structures are reproduced. The experiences of teachers who are seeking promotion (first into middle management then into senior management positions in schools, with a headship as the ultimate goal for a few) work to reproduce the established career ladder for teachers. When the headteacher position is achieved, however, then there is discontinuity for some heads between their expectations and their experiences and understandings about career. For some headteachers, perhaps a majority, their experiences of career beyond headship reproduce no structure since there is no generally acknowledged career ladder for headteachers other than to remain in their first headship position. For some heads, the structure of careers and the culture of their experiences and expectations are at variance.

The analysis of the concept of career undertaken in Chapter 2 can assist in understanding the nature of the problem for headteachers. From the perspective of the organization (Gunz, 1989), career structures are part of the process by means of which in England organizations like local authority educational systems renew themselves, and employers (currently LEAs) maintain people-flow. Career structures are the salary and promotional ladders which are developed in organizations (schools) and professions such as teaching whereby employees and practitioners are allocated to different posts and positions of responsibility. By seeking promotion, the flow of people between positions is maintained, the schools are staffed and the local authority educational organization is renewed.

Over the past thirty years or so, there has been an increase in the development and elaboration of career structures within organizations and professions in general. Career structures have been developed, often by careers consultants, usually controlled by employers and governments, with the intention of securing workers (such as teachers) commitment and motivation. Thus by working to develop their careers and achieve promotion, teachers are at the same time meeting the needs of the local educational authority for committed practitioners and enthusiastic employees. If headteachers have no career structure, therefore, it is possible that, for some, their commitment and enthusiasm might diminish over time since there is no further career goal to which they can aspire. The employers of teachers and headteachers need to consider the issue of careers in education, therefore, since commitment and motivation are essential qualities for senior management position holders.

It is important to remember, however, the duality of structure and the logical entailment of structure and action (Giddens, 1981). Career structures are renewed and reproduced by individuals accepting and following organizationally defined career routes and paths. We must not underestimate the influence of career builders in the construction of career ladders. Individuals do increase their chances of promotion success by following already proven career routes. But careers are not physical structures even though they have structural properties (Giddens, 1981; Gunz, 1989). Neither are career structures permanent; they are constantly being changed and modified. They are reality-defining for teachers and other employees in that they do both constrain and enable action (Giddens, 1984). But, nevertheless, career structures are maintained and reproduced or modified and changed by the actions of teachers and headteachers themselves.

If this model of career structure and individuals' actions is correct then the implications for headteachers who are concerned about the lack of further promotion structures or transferability between structures become clearer. If large numbers of headteachers continue to remain in their first headship posts, then this becomes the generally accepted and acknowledged career pattern for heads. Only by large numbers of heads moving out, transferring to other schools or other structures, convincing employers and thereby developing and eventually establishing career routes for headteachers, will a career structure for heads emerge and become accepted.

The difficulties for individual headteachers and for pathfinders have to be acknowledged. In England there have always been a small number of heads who have moved on to become advisers, inspectors, LEA or even DES administrators, college principals or directors, or researchers. But small numbers cannot form a promotion ladder or a career structure. Career patterns can be changed and new career structures can be formed only if sufficient individuals choose a different route. Groups of individuals can exert an influence on career structures. Gunz (1989) considered a number of ways in which individuals' career action might affect organizational promotion structures. Also, it is important to consider the collective response. Of how through established political channels (trade unions and professional associations) as well as through informal alliances, pacts and groupings, collective action can (sometimes) influence, affect and re-define career structures and systems. If headteacher trade unions and professional associations are made to recognize the career concerns of some of their members, then such concerns will be represented and voiced to teachers' employers, and perhaps more widely.

It is also important to emphasize the opportunities (as well as the constraints) which wider, externally-imposed change might offer for the creation and alteration of career and promotion ladders in teaching. In England changes such as LMS, the opting-out of schools from LEA control and the possibility of a change of employer from local to central government give an opportunity for teachers' and headteachers' associations to think about the structure of careers in education. New administrative and managerial positions are bound to be created. Career structures and ladders *have* to change when positions in organizations are not being filled. Wider changes, as well as expansion, can mean a modification of the 'rules' which govern who gets particular positions. When organizations change, new patterns of people-flow have to emerge and develop into modified and adjusted career structures and ladders.

In the same way, career structures and ladders for headteachers will develop if new administrative and managerial positions are created or established posts are not being filled. But only when sufficient numbers of headteachers alter the established pattern (of remaining in a headship post), via their actions and their demands, will new career structures emerge and become established career patterns. Changes currently under way in education might constitute a 'window of opportunity' for the development of new career structures for headteachers. But only by understanding how career actions can affect career structures (as well as understanding how structures limit and constrain actions) can the structures that seem to define the experiences of headteacher career be modified and changed.

Chapter 9

The New Headteacher

Changes to the headteacher role have been a common theme in sociological and educational research (Peters, 1976; Earley and Weindling, 1987). It is recognized that the role of the head is becoming increasingly diverse and complex (Fullan, 1992). The expansion of managerial and executive tasks and the reduction in educational leadership aspects have also been documented (Morgan, Hall and Mackay, 1983; Evetts, 1991). There has been discussion of the changing role of headship as a result of recent educational legislation in Britain. Under local financial management of schools, and where schools opt for grant-maintained status, then headteachers are more obviously influential and have more scope to plan and to control their schools' resources and expenditures (Levacic, 1989). Some researchers have argued that the role change for headteachers will be less than that of many of the other participants in the running of schools, such as governors and LEA officials (Hill, Oakley Smith and Spinks, 1990, p. 66). This chapter will argue that the changes to the headteacher role have been very significant. It will demonstrate that the contexts and opportunities for micro-political activity in schools have been increased. It will show that the orientation of the headteacher's work role has been dramatically changed. It will argue that the work culture of headship has been fundamentally altered, resulting in major transformations in the structural determinants of careers in teaching and head-ship in Britain. Finally, the theme of career structures and career action is returned to in the context of these changes to the headteacher role.

The secondary headteachers whose career history accounts have illustrated the themes of this book were contacted again in the autumn of 1992. A question-naire invited them to comment on particular aspects of their experiences of head-ship in the previous two years since the original interviews. These responses are used in this examination of the changing role of headship.

Of the twenty heads, eighteen responded. In the interim period three heads had retired, one prematurely as a result of a school closure. Other than these retirements, the heads' personal circumstances had not changed, except one (male) head was experiencing a period of 'second parenthood' with the birth of his two baby sons. Changes to their schools were more common, however. One school had been closed. Two schools were at various stages of seeking grant-maintained status. All schools were managing formula-funded budgets, some with historic funding supplements. Five schools had had an increase in pupil numbers; one a reduction in pupil intake as a result of parents choosing alternative schools.

REDIRECTING AND EXPANDING MICRO-POLITICAL ACTIVITIES

The headteachers' accounts indicated a redirection of micro-political negotiations and an increase in such activities. The *change* in direction will be illustrated using the heads' accounts of their negotiations over staffing. The *increase* in micro-political activity will be demonstrated by means of the heads' accounts of their relations with governing bodies.

Negotiations over Staffing: Changing the Participants

In England micro-political negotiations in respect of staffing have always formed an important part of a headteacher's job. Until recently, LEA formulas for determining staffing levels, using schools' unit totals and hence groupings, always left room for negotiation in respect of curriculum coverage, special needs, catchment areas, particular initiatives, and so on. Prior to LMS, negotiations were between heads, often together with their curriculum deputies, and the LEA area education officer. Mrs Selby's account of the ground-rules for such micro-political negotiations was typical of all the heads' experiences prior to LMS:

> Before formula funding, every year in September, every
> secondary school had to fill in a form known as an SCD form.
> Basically that was a record of all the staff, what they taught,
> how many periods, what level, and so on. It was a record of
> every period taught to every year group, and it was also a
> prediction of the number of teaching periods per subject we
> envisaged we were going to need for the next five years.
>   Now those used to be filled in in September and sent in to
> the authority and in due course in the mid autumn term the head
> and very often, as in our case, the deputy, who'd actually filled
> them in, would go along for an interview usually with the area
> education officer or his representative and a phase inspector. We
> would discuss this return and discuss the way that we were
> using staff and whether we had an options pattern that was
> costly in use of staff in 4th and 5th years, how many children we
> had in our year groups and class groups, and how we provided
> for special needs, etc, etc. At the end of the discussion the area
> officer would say 'Right, well on our reckoning for next year,
> you're going to need X number of teacher periods and with

regard to the form that you're using for the curriculum then we reckon you would need Y number of teachers to cover it'. And we would then quibble a bit over this and we would come eventually to some sort of agreement as to what the staffing figure that they were recommending might be. They would then recommend that to the authority. Now of course the area education person was looking at it in terms of their area. The authority people were looking at it in terms of the global county figure. The county would generally cut it down by one or one-point-five, sometimes more. And it would then filter back through to us. That wasn't the end of the story because we would hear that figure about March or April and come June when we were struggling with the timetable I, in our case, would go, start with the telephone and finish up in person, with the local education officer saying 'Look we just can't cover that', or 'We've got so many pupils wanting to do that in the 4th year', or 'Although we've got this number of staff, we haven't got enough people, where there's flexibility to cover that subject', or whatever. Sometimes I could wheedle successfully and persuade or sometimes the pupil numbers would go up for the first year. You know, all sorts of things could happen. He would have a certain flexibility within the city and he could say 'Yes, go on then'. Sometimes he'd still say 'No, I can't'. So then I'd have to go through the same process at County Hall and again sometimes I was lucky and sometimes I wasn't.

(Mrs Selby)

Under LMS, staffing levels are constrained by budget allocations rather than by LEA-defined staffing formulas. However, LEA periods of transition and the retention of historic supplements gave heads a breathing space in which to balance their budgets. The career history heads were anticipating some of the problems and in doing so the re-direction of micro-political negotiations into schools, and away from LEAs, was apparent. Learning the new micro-political rules was causing problems for some heads who had been particularly successful in negotiations in the past with their LEA. Miss Reeves explained her difficulties as resulting in part from her successes in past negotiations.

Before LMS the authority determined how many teachers you could have, partly on tradition and partly on what you could argue out of your local area officer and then what he could argue out of county. We used to argue for very high staffing because we were a deprived catchment area and county supported us in that. In addition we supplemented out of the TVEI initiative because we were one of the five schools that piloted that. And that kept two or three teachers going....

> Under LMS we stood to be in great difficulty because our
> staff are now, well the bulk of them, are at or near the top of the
> scale. Also we have very inflated staffing because I'd been very
> good at negotiating extra staff out of the authority. That's a
> talent I should have lost!
>
> (Miss Reeves)

Under LMS micro-political activities over staffing have been redirected, away from headteacher-LEA negotiations to within-school negotiations. The new parties in micro-political bargaining in schools over staff numbers are headteachers, senior management (particularly budget managers) and governors. Extracts from the headteachers' accounts illustrated the changes in the negotiating teams and the new ground rules for negotiation:

> Whereas the LEA last year would have said you are having
> seventy-two teachers, non-negotiable, but we will argue about
> one or two. But come next April the governors will determine
> how many teachers we are having.
>
> (Mr Bennett)

> We wanted the best person for the job and if she was the best
> person then we must appoint her. We must find the money from
> somewhere. But then I've got a budget manager saying 'We can't
> go on saying we're going to find the money from somewhere. I
> can't you know, I've found all the money that I can find'.
>
> (Mrs Green)

The new rules for micro-political bargaining were budgetary rather than time-honoured and widely accepted justifications, such as educational need and catchment area difficulties. The new negotiating parties were within-school rather than school–LEA deliberations.

Headteachers have always been required to make difficult decisions over staffing: shedding 'surplus' staff if school rolls fall, and recruiting and retaining staff to fill vacancies have always involved difficult decisions. Mr Clifford's account demonstrated how some of the career history heads saw advantages under LMS in enabling them more easily to reward and retain deserving staff. However, the redirection of such negotiations within the school, and the increased influence of heads, other senior management and governors in such negotiations were apparent.

> By and large I would say the results are beneficial in the sense
> that we have more freedom to do some of the things that we
> have always wanted to do. I can in fact say, I want those two
> ladies put on scale four and it happens, providing the chairman
> of governors agrees. Or if I say I want one on three and one on
> five, that will happen and I am no longer bound by the

bureaucracy at County Hall saying, 'Oh no, in your size of school it has to be a two and a three'. That is a great relief.

(Mr Clifford)

In terms of headteachers' negotiations over staffing, therefore, LMS has maintained the extent of such activities but changed the parties in the negotiations, and in the process has probably given heads more influence, although budget constraints are very real. Bargaining between heads and LEA administrators over staffing have been replaced by within-school negotiations between heads, senior managers and governors, constrained by budgetary allocations. Such a change makes even more urgent an appreciation of the various ways in which power is exercised in schools. Ball (1987) has argued that we should not *assume* consensus and legitimacy in respect of the authority of the headteacher. Instead we should try to expose the interpersonal influences, the compromises and the bargaining that are part of the operation of schools, as of all other complex organizations. If the context for some micro-political activity is now even more focused within schools themselves, then we need to understand more about the operation of such activities.

Relations with Governing Bodies: Increasing Micro-Political Activities

The change to LMS has increased the opportunities for and is gradually expanding the areas of micro-political activities in schools. The career history headteachers were asked about relationships with their governing bodies in the original interview and then two years later in the follow-up questionnaire. In terms of such relationships, LMS provided new and increased opportunities for micro-political negotiation.

The original interviews had shown the heads' experiences with their newly empowered governing bodies to have been variable. Some reported their governors' willingness to accept unquestioningly the head's recommendations and a reluctance to query his/her wishes. Others found governors more independent and stressed the practical consequences, in particular the extended timescale needed for coming to decisions. What was clear, however, was the increase in the amount of negotiation that was required in attempting to operationalize arrangements with the newly constituted and empowered governing bodies.

The governors are finding now that they can't cope with the work. They have set up sub-committees so they can divide the work up through sub-committees. That's throwing a lot of strain on us because to service the working sub-committees demands a higher level of input from ourselves and that is far more frequent. I mean a governing body used to meet, what, once every two months and now it meets once every six weeks and

there is a sub-committee meeting every week. I or my
deputies or other senior staff are always attending a
sub-committee, week in and week out. The committees quite
rightly need promoting, they need guidance, knowledge.
Basically they ask questions, they set up whole trains of
information which they don't want divided from the meeting,
which then has to be serviced. So there is a huge work load
developing with the relationship of the governing body which is
not just LMS inspired, it's inspired through their responsibilities
for the National Curriculum as well, but a lot of it is LMS. So
whereas in the past I would have simply said, 'Right Mr X has
left us, a scientist, we need a replacement scientist', the process
of making that decision is now more with the governing body
rather than me doing it on my own. That sets up all sorts of
dimensions of time and negotiation.

(Mr Bennett)

In Mr Bennett's account, he explained the increase in the numbers of
meetings and the need to service such meetings with information. Other headteachers in the group were anticipating management problems, largely because,
with the increased powers of governors, the heads' authority would not necessarily go unchallenged. The extracts from Mrs Peters' and Mrs Selby's accounts
were representative of some of the headteachers' concerns:

There is the difficulty of managing the management of it by the
governors and involving them to the appropriate extent without
letting them slow down the whole process of running a school.
That I think is going to be a major problem because if you
conscientiously try and involve them at every stage it's very
difficult not to slow it down, almost impossible. I think that's
going to be a real problem. You cannot, with the best will in the
world, as a governor step into a school like this and understand
the intricacies of how and why the Sixth Form Centre is staffed.
It's taken me a long time. You can't start pulling holes in the
secondary curriculum and time-table and say 'Can't we
economize?' You can't do that.

(Mrs Peters)

I'm very fortunate that I have a governing body which still
generally takes the line 'Your job is to run the school and our job
is to help you'. If I had a governing body that said our job is to
run the school and your job is to do what we tell you, then LMS
would make it infinitely more difficult. As it is the governors
take not just my advice but the school's advice. They have their
ideas, they are very, very able. We've got a very good Finance

Committee with people on it who are in business, or are
accountants, so we've got people there who are very
knowledgeable and can comprehend large sums of money far
better than I can. I am very fortunate but I can imagine that for
some heads who have not been pilot schools, who have not got
governing bodies like mine, they are either going to be
governing bodies of people who are well-intentioned but totally
without experience or ability in these matters or, which may
even be worse, those who think they know an awful lot about
schools and who think they can run it in a full way. Now there I
think it must be almost impossible.

(Mrs Selby)

The necessity to negotiate with governing bodies and sub-committees
expanded the opportunities for micro-political activity, for interpersonal
influence, compromise and bargaining. The chances of conflict were thereby
increased; heads could not assume their recommendations would go unchallenged or that consensus would always result.

In the follow-up questionnaire study such increases in the opportunities for
micro-politics were confirmed. All the headteachers commented on the greatly
increased workload and on the need to attend more and longer meetings. Some
governing bodies had introduced sub-committees to deal with particular responsibilities such as Personnel, Finance, Premises and Community, and General
Purposes. All committees and sub-committees needed servicing with information and school policies had to be discussed and negotiated and argued through.
It was generally felt that decision-making was slower both because of the
increased extent of negotiations over policies and because of the need to cross-
check policies (objectives and intermediate measures) against changing legal
requirements.

The chances of conflict in such negotiations were also increasing. In the
follow-up questionnaire most of the heads were as yet unconcerned since they
felt their advice and recommendations were usually followed. But four heads had
commented specifically on the emergence of certain tensions in their relations
with their governing bodies. Sometimes the heads' authority had been under-
mined; sometimes the interventionist stance of some governors was beginning
to be felt. One head had commented on the number of in-quorate committee
meetings which gave more opportunities for the Clerk of Governors to claim to
represent the views of the governing body. Wherever heads and parent governors were united over policy matters (e.g. over the introduction of a school
uniform, a decision that went against LEA policy), then the increased power of
governing bodies was welcomed by the heads. The heads were becoming increasingly aware, however, that their recommendations would not always go unchallenged and consensus would not always result. Micro-political activities and
negotiations were increasing and expanding.

CHANGING THE ORIENTATION OF THE HEADSHIP ROLE

The changes in the criteria used to select and appoint headteachers have already been discussed (Chapter 4). The experiences of the heads in this study show that educational philosophy and leadership abilities are becoming less important as the need for managerial skills increase. Here, the headteachers' accounts of their increased control of maintenance and running costs and their new responsibilities for generating income illustrate the change of orientation that is being required.

Maintenance and Running Costs

An amount for the maintenance and running costs of school premises is included in formula funding, which heads and governing bodies can allocate according to their views of priorities. One year into LMS, the heads in this study were not entirely clear how this would work. They saw advantages in getting work done when the school wanted it and could afford it, but realized the sum allocated was small, thus giving little real choice. The rules governing virement were unclear at the time of the original interviews. Mr Bennett's account illustrates the different arrangements under LMS compared with LEA-controlled maintenance schemes, and the extract from Miss Reeves' account demonstrates the perceived advantages:

> If you take painting as an example. The LEA would have said this is your painting programme; we have determined it on a budget owned and controlled by us and it's three classrooms a year and in March; which three classrooms do you want painting? I would look at their records at what was painted and when. I would note that room hasn't been painted for nine years and that one for nine years and that one for ten years, so we'll have those three done. And then the following year they'd come again and say we'll do four this year, which four do you want? Oh the school hall has had a lot of wear-and-tear this last year, we'll do that.
>
> But now all those decisions are going to be the decisions of the governing body against a budget. That opens up all sorts of areas of argument and disagreement.
>
> (Mr Bennett)

> I inherited a telephone system which was out of the ark, I won't tell you its various deficiencies it would take too long but it is useless. BT charges a vast sum for this hideous nonsense which was designed to prevent communication. Now I have been

looking round at various companies and I've got one at least who say they will be able to install and let us pay for a new system for less than what BT is renting the rubbish for. And I have been, for the last 11 years, trying to get a new system out of County Hall. I've been told: oh it's somebody else's department; we'll put you on the list; yes you're on the list; we'll send Mr X out; Mr X will come; perhaps we'll put it in next year's budget; and so on for 11 solid years! Now within a year I am going to get a telephone system that actually works and it'll be cheaper than the one that I'm ditching. So that is very welcome.

(Miss Reeves)

However, several of the headteachers recognized the limits to their powers imposed by the budget itself. In addition, in the transition period, arrangements made by one LEA had worked to postpone, and might even prevent, full powers over maintenance and running costs going to the schools:

I can see the value of the head and the governors managing their own maintenance budgets, but you've got to have those resources to manage!

(Mrs Morley)

In theory we are able to make our own decisions about painting and decorating. But painting and repairs haven't been happening. From having no say over it at all, we now have total control over it, but we have to find the money to do it!

(Mrs Green)

The authority has already taken on board a number of contracts that are going to last for 4 years, for example the cleaning contract which to date has not been very successful because it went to the local authority itself and it would appear that they made some mistakes in the contract. But we are going to have to stick by that for 4 years. Before we get LMS next year they are going to have established a catering contract. There is also set up and in part working a contract for school grounds. They have also taken on a number of contracts with suppliers and it is the contract with suppliers that a school as large as this sometimes works to its disadvantage in that we have to buy off the county list. I know full well we could have contracts on copiers that would have been more advantageous to ourselves. We have to understand that the county contract protects the smaller schools so that they are gaining in the same way we are, but we are not gaining quite as much as we could if we went our own way.

(Mr Hall)

In general the heads welcomed the increased control of maintenance and running costs afforded by LMS. Two years later, in the follow-up study, this aspect of LMS was still very much appreciated. All the heads applauded the greater control, the flexibility and freedom, and the opportunity to prioritize. The rules concerning virement were now clear and the heads and their governing bodies could more easily respond to the needs and improve the environment of their respective schools. The heads felt in control of institutional maintenance and upkeep, though a few still commented on the underfunding and the time taken to put contracts out for tender. But in general this aspect of the principle of devolved management received widespread approval. It did, however, represent a significant change in the way headteachers used their working time.

> There is no doubt in my mind that we are now into school
> development planning and as part of that we are heavily into
> planning cycles. If you take just premises, [all maintenance
> projects] are the decisions of the governing body against a
> budget. So in terms of the upkeep of the premises you've got to
> have a five-year progressive planning cycle that says a set of
> classroom furniture has a five-year life; a set of tables and chairs
> is £1,500; therefore to keep abreast of what we need, we need to
> be spending £6,000 on the cycle of classroom furniture renewal
> (for one classroom). And that is just one planning cycle, there are
> many others.
>
> (Mr Bennett)

Income Generation in Schools

Under LMS, formula-funded budgets for schools are based to a large extent on numbers of pupils and their ages (age-weighted pupil units). Some schools, particularly in the transition period, have received extra allocations for special needs and historic differences. More important in the long term, however, is the fact that extra resources can now be earned by schools as a result of income-generating activities. Such activities can bring direct financial benefit. Heads, their senior management teams and governing bodies are having to think in commercial terms. They are increasingly engaging in negotiations with industrial and commercial organizations in order to expand their resources. They are renting out their buildings and charging for services. They are seeking sponsorship from industry and local business for both capital expenditure and to meet running costs. The need to develop public relations and to promote the interests of their schools as financial enterprises are stimulating new skills in heads and senior managers.

The career history heads' responses to this change were mixed. All recognized the necessity for such activities but in general they were reluctant to welcome them. A degree of professional scepticism seemed to be required. An extract from Mrs Ince's account illustrated the general reluctance:

> Although I do take public relations seriously and in that sense presenting a school as I think it truly is, in a good light, I do not think it is my job to take people out to lunch and all that kind of thing. That is one of the reasons why I was never interested in a career in business because that is not a way I wish to spend my time. However, when I talk to people I know in other fields, they seem to think that possibly is the way a headteacher in the future ought to spend his or her time. It is not something that I welcome, no, my interest in it is managing well the resources that I have, not pouring out time and energy into persuading someone to give me more.
>
> (Mrs Ince)

Such reluctance apart, the expansion of financial negotiations both inside and outside schools was acknowledged as important. Mrs Peters, a newly appointed head, though not necessarily welcoming the new commercialism, was actively seeking out and developing income-generating and self-help activities:

> There's nothing in our estimates for capital development. What I'm saying to the governors is we can't have any capital development on a budget like this and County Hall doesn't allow for that. We've got to find sponsorship and I'll handle that with my contacts in the business world. And it's not a one-off thing; I'm looking for about £30,000 every year minimum because I don't see how we can develop without it because money isn't going to come from anywhere else. That's got to be a major part of my effort I think, because otherwise we won't get new suites of rooms, the place will run down, we won't be able to afford to refurbish the theatre, we'll never restock the library. We're lucky in that we've had the information technology project from county but we won't be able to keep it up if we don't get that sort of money from outside. So I think it's madness to ignore that. Already we've done quite well, we've got something approaching £30,000 sponsorship from DTI; it's for a very specific project, a bar-coding project, a stock control project. I mean there are lots of other benefits, links with industry and so on.
>
> We've raised several hundred pounds from an all-night disco specifically for school funds. We do something which I suspect is quite illegal and ask them to give a donation when they join. I suppose I might get away with it again. A local firm donated the new econet cable for the computer system. You just have to be always on the look-out for things. We're investing in equipment

that is high cost but is a more effective use of labour in the
ancillary staff, so we bought a fax machine, we bought an
improved reprographics facility. We're trying to do things that
speed things up, make things run more smoothly and more
effectively. I think we have to look at those sort of ways of
saving labour, glass-washing machines in science, all those sort
of things you have to be aware of and look at.

We do a lot of self-help repairs, a lot of self-help
redecorating, inside even, and I think we've got to do more of
that. We had an environment week and cleaned the whole site of
litter. It's a very vulnerable site with rights of way through it
and the Sports Centre open all the time; nice pleasant place to
walk your dog. But we got the whole place cleaned up, a self-help
generated campaign just before half-term. I think you can't let
up on any of those sort of things if you want the sort of
environment that children deserve to be educated in.

(Mrs Peters)

Thus headteachers' management skills are no longer confined to within-
school and school–LEA bargaining; they must increasingly create opportunities for seeking aid from industry and commerce in order to expand resources.
These constitute new orientations and areas of work for headteachers in
Britain.

THE NEW HEADTEACHER

In what ways have the extension of micro-political activity in schools and the
changes in the orientation of headteachers' work created a new kind of headteacher? Again an answer can be sought in the experiences of the career history
heads. In general the headteachers welcomed LMS and the advantages were
thought to outweigh the disadvantages. However, in the follow-up study, all the
headteachers could list several important ways in which their work had changed
in the last few years. Most commented on the increased workload, the greater
complexity of management and administration, the need for new skills and the
lack of any appropriate training. Other headteachers identified major differences in their experiences of day-to-day work.

I'm becoming a computer buff. I didn't think that's what
headship involved.

(Mr Oakes)

Running LMS is putting a gulf between me and the school.

(Mrs Grainger)

It's a waste of a deputy head's and headteacher's time and
educational skills.

(Miss Hollis)

I'm experiencing a growing feeling of isolation.

(Mr Stevens)

Schools are encouraged to compete rather than cooperate. Pupils
mean additional finance.

(Mr Hall)

The LEA has been marginalized so there is no strategic
planning. Everything is down to individual schools. In times of
financial stringency, cuts and redundancies are seen as the fault
of individual schools and political responsibility is less clearly
attributable.

(Mrs Ince)

In terms of day-to-day work activities, headteachers were more completely
managers and administrators. Their need to forward plan for their separate
individual schools, to keep up with the mountains of paperwork (forms, reports
and proposals), and the need to match up calendar, financial and academic considerations, meant that they were more completely office-bound. Contact with
pupils was becoming minimal and contact with teaching colleagues, other than
senior management, was considerably reduced. Heads were becoming isolated;
a gulf was growing between manager-heads and the school organizations they
were administering. In addition, heads were becoming isolated from other headteachers. Competition between schools was increasing feelings of isolation. Success for one school in recruiting additional pupils meant failure for another
school. Worries were increasing about general and special education provision
and about particular schools' special needs. Thus schools with large, extensive
grounds, schools experiencing increased criminal activity and vandalism, and
schools with large numbers of pupils with parents in difficulties, felt that their
particular needs were not being addressed by formula-funding arrangements.

The removal or weakening of LEA provisioning was increasing anxieties
about isolation as well as heightening uncertainties about future changes and
the effects on budgets. The new headteacher was required to be able to maintain
boundaries around what were appropriate managerial work tasks and what were
not; what was involved in corporate management and what was peripheral. If
in the past headteachers had been generalists in their educational leadership
roles, displaying a managerialist concern for students and their staff colleagues,
they were increasingly required to become finance and strategy specialists,
thereby shifting the focus of the work culture of headship (Simkins et al., 1992).
The consequences of such changes for careers in teaching are extensive and
fundamental.

CAREER STRUCTURES AND CAREER ACTION

Styles of management, administration and professionalism change: in both private and public organizations, those styles that are encouraged and considered effective at one time may not be so at another (Scase and Goffee, 1989). As a result, the qualities and characteristics expected to be displayed by those individuals who are developing careers and seeking promotion are also subject to change. Individuals at middle-ranking and even more at senior levels in the 1990s are expected to adopt work practices, goals and objectives which are quite different from those regarded as more appropriate in the 1950s and 1960s (McCrone, Elliott and Bechhofer, 1989).

In the 1960s those achieving promotion in the career, particularly in the public sector, were expected to develop management styles which were people-centred; problems were discussed, decision-making was shared and policies were jointly owned; control was cooperative and by agreement rather than directive. The characteristics required of those seeking promotion into managerial positions (in both public and private organizations) in the 1980s and 1990s are different. The new styles, often attributed to Thatcherite conviction rather than consensus politics (Marwick, 1982; Kavanagh, 1987), emphasize the need for competition, personal assertiveness, firm leadership and strong control (Scase and Goffee, 1989). These are the characteristics of corporate managerialism (Simkins *et al.*, 1992).

These changes have affected public services such as education, social services and health as well as private industry. There are career implications for professional as well as for occupational workers. Both public and private sector organizations are required to become more 'cost-effective' and 'efficient'. In general this is to be achieved by 'decentralization' (Morgan, 1986), by giving more autonomy to parts and sections through devolved systems of budgetary control and then confining and limiting the autonomy through increased competition, performance-related monitoring and appraisal schemes (Scase and Goffee, 1989). Individuals seeking or achieving promotion in the new-style organizations, both public and private, are required constantly to demonstrate their competence and effectiveness and to achieve higher levels of measurable performance.

Careers in teaching have followed such changes and have undergone dramatic transformations. The career and salary structure for all teachers was altered in 1987. The replacement of the old system of scale posts with a basic salary scale and incentive allowances means that careers in teaching are less predictable and automatic (Scase and Goffee, 1989, would claim less bureaucratic). Promotion in teaching now depends more on the distribution of managerial tasks and responsibilities in particular schools. The efficient execution of work related to teaching, appropriate experience and even the possession of additional qualifications are no longer sufficient for obtaining promotion. Instead, fixed-term salary incentives are offered for doing particular jobs in schools, as rewards for effort, accountability, extra responsibilities and performance-related achievements. As a result, senior managers in schools hope to achieve organizational flexibility, lower operating costs and improved motivation and commitment from junior staff (Stewart, 1986).

The devolution of budgetary control as well as the option of grant-maintained status has dramatically differentiated the work of senior managers in schools from the work of classroom teachers. Throughout the 1980s the effects of change on teachers' status, particularly their status as professionals, had been a significant issue. Ozga (1981) used the term 'proletarianization' and Apple (1982) used the term 'deskilling' to refer to the erosion of teachers' skill and autonomy in the classroom. The increase in managerial control which has tended to make classroom teachers 'workers' while heads and deputies are 'managers' had also been discussed (Lawn and Grace, 1987; Burgess, 1984; Gillborn, 1989). These changes have been accelerated and expanded following the 1988 Education Reform Act. The extent of change has rendered old debates about teaching as a profession (Leggatt, 1970) and even about the effect women have on a profession's status (Simpson and Simpson, 1969) less and less relevant (Acker, 1983).

The 1988 Education Act promoted institutional competitiveness between schools in their recruitment of pupils in giving parents more opportunity to choose schools for their children. Formula-funded budgets are largely determined by numbers of pupils on roll. In addition, schools have been encouraged to seek sponsorship from commerce and industry for particular projects and in order to increase the amounts they receive in addition to their formula-funded budgets.

The new headteacher role now includes important elements of corporate managerialism. Heads have to be *measurably* efficient and effective managers of their individual schools. Emphasis is placed on their directional skills and their ability to motivate staff to achieve national curriculum objectives and pupil assessment targets (Hunt, 1986). Such skills are arguably different from the leadership skills which were in vogue in the 1970s (Simkins *et al.*, 1992). In addition, in controlling their own budgets heads and senior managers in schools require accountancy and computing skills and the ability to be tough, even aggressive, in negotiations with governing bodies. Heads have to be competitive in their recruitment of pupils and emphasize school achievements in their attempts to influence parents. The pressures on headteachers and the resultant stresses (Ostell and Oakland, 1993) are increasing as heads are required to be more directive and autocratic in their styles of management (NFER, 1989).

For headteachers who are also women, corporate managerialism is likely to highlight the cultural contradictions that abound for women in senior management positions (Evetts, 1994). Corporate managerialism seems to give prominence to qualities such as efficiency, accountability, ambition, striving and competition. At the same time, qualities such as caring, nurturing, loyalty and cooperation are difficult to measure and hence difficult to reward. Yet these are precisely the qualities that have made promotion in the teaching career attractive to many women and men. One consequence of the new headteacher role might be a further increase in gender, as well as other, differences in headteacher postholders in British schools.

It is important to end by restating the principle of structuration (Chapter 2): of how career structures emerge and are reproduced or changed by career actions. The structural determinants of and constraints on careers and promotions in teaching are real and formidable. Thus if those seeking promotion in teaching support a people-centred style of leadership and management when those in control of resources and promotion positions (increasingly heads as well as governors of individual schools) are requiring more assertive and task-centred styles, then such individuals (men and women) are unlikely to achieve promotion to senior management. Alternatively, new career structures might develop, say into pastoral and deputy head positions, for those wishing to develop particular qualities of leadership such as care, nurturance and people-centred styles. Variation in routes gives choice to individuals as well as enabling styles of management, administration and professionalism to change yet again as new ideologies of 'competence' and 'high performance', and new key values and issues emerge and gain credence. One consequence might be occupational segregation by gender or the development of dead-end career positions in promotion terms. But it is necessary to emphasize that career actions *can* alter structures just as structures affect and constrain career actions. The focus on change is essential therefore. Only by beginning to understand how career structures in teaching and headship change and are changed, does it become possible to devise career actions that are appropriate for changing career structures.

Bibliography

Abrams, P. (1982) *Historical Sociology*. Shepton Mallet: Open Books.

Acker, S. (1980) Women, the other academics. *British Journal of Sociology of Education*, 1 (1): 68–80.

Acker, S. (1983) Women and teaching: a semi-detached sociology of a semi-profession. In S. Walker and L. Barton (eds), *Gender, Class and Education*. Lewes: Falmer Press.

Acker, S. (1987) Primary school teaching as an occupation. In S. Delamont (ed.), *The Primary School Teacher*. Lewes: Falmer Press.

Acker, S. (1988) Teachers, gender and resistance. *British Journal of Sociology of Education*, 9 (3): 307–22.

Acker, S. (1989) (ed.) *Teachers, Gender and Careers*. Lewes: Falmer Press.

Adams, N. (1987) *Secondary School Management Today*. London: Hutchinson Education.

Adkison, J. (1981) Women in school administration. A review of the literature. *Review of Educational Research*, 51 (3): 311–43.

Allan, G. (1979) *A Sociology of Friendship and Kinship*. London: Allen & Unwin.

Allen, B. (1968) *Headship in the 1970s*. Oxford: Blackwell.

Apple, M. W. (ed.) (1982) *Cultural and Economic Reproduction in Education*. London: Routledge & Kegan Paul.

Archer, J. and Lloyd, B. (1982) *Sex and Gender*. Harmondsworth: Penguin.

Atkinson, P. (1981) *The Clinical Experience*. Farnborough: Gower.

Atkinson, P. and Delamont, S. (1985) Socialization into teaching. *British Journal of Sociology of Education*, 6 (3): 307–22.

Auld, R. (1976) *Report on the Inquiry into William Tyndale School*. London: Inner London Education Authority.

Ball, S. J. (1981) *Beachside Comprehensive*. Cambridge: Cambridge University Press.

Ball, S. J. (1987) *The Micro-Politics of the School*. London and New York: Methuen.

Ball, S. J. and Goodson, I. F. (eds) (1985) *Teachers' Lives and Careers*. Lewes: Falmer Press.

Barry, C. H. and Tye, F. (1972) *Running a School*. London: Temple Smith.

Becker, H. S., Geer, B., Hughes, E. C. and Strauss, A. L. (1961) *Boys in White*. Chicago: Chicago University Press.

Bennet, C. (1985) Paints, pots or promotion: art teachers' attitudes towards their careers. In S. J. Ball and I. F. Goodson (eds), *Teachers' Lives and Careers*. Lewes: Falmer Press.

Berg, L. (1968) *Risinghill: The Death of a Comprehensive School*. Harmondsworth: Penguin.

Berger, P. L. and Luckmann, T. (1967) *The Social Construction of Reality*. London: Allen Lane/ Penguin.

Bertaux, D. (1981) *Biography and Society*. London: Sage.

Beynon, J. (1985) Institutional change and career histories in a comprehensive school. In S. J. Ball and I. F. Goodson (eds) *Teachers' Lives and Careers*. Lewes: Falmer Press.

Blumberg, A. and Greenfield, W. (1980) *The Effective Principal: Perspectives in School Leadership*. Boston: Allyn & Bacon.

Bott, E. (1957, new edition, 1971) *Family and Social Network*. London: Tavistock.

Bourdieu, P. (1976) Marriage strategies as strategies of social reproduction. In E. Forster and P. M. Ranum (eds), *Family and Society*. Baltimore: Johns Hopkins University Press.

Burgess, R. G. (1982) *Field Research: A Sourcebook and Field Manual*. London: Allen & Unwin.

Burgess, R. G. (1983) *Experiencing Comprehensive Education: A Study of Bishop McGregor School*. London: Methuen.

Burgess, R. G. (1984a) Autobiographical accounts and research experience. In R. G. Burgess (ed.), *The Research Process in Educational Settings: Ten Case Studies*. Lewes: Falmer Press.

Burgess, R. G. (1984b) Headship: freedom or constraint? In S. J. Ball (ed.), *Comprehensive Schooling: A Reader*. Lewes: Falmer Press.

Burgess, R. G. (1985a) (ed.) *Field Methods in the Study of Education*. Lewes: Falmer Press.

Burgess, R. G. (1985b) (ed.) *Strategies of Educational Research: Qualitative Methods*. Lewes: Falmer Press.

Burgess, R. G. (1985c) (ed.) *Issues in Educational Research: Qualitative Methods*. Lewes: Falmer Press.

Burgess, R. G. (1986) *Sociology, Education and Schools*. London: Batsford.

Bush, T. (1989) *Managing Education: Theory and Practice*. Milton Keynes: Open University Press.

Byrne, E. (1978) *Women and Education*. London: Tavistock.

Callon, M. and Latour, B. (1981) Unscrewing the big Leviathan. In K. Knorr-Cetina and A. V. Cicourel (eds), *Advances in Social Theory and Methodology*. Boston and London: Routledge & Kegan Paul.

Chapman, J. B. (1978) Male and female leadership styles – the double bind. In J. A. Ramaley (ed.), *Covert Discrimination and Women in the Sciences*. Boulder, CO: Westview Press.

Cicourel, A. V. (1981) Notes on the integration of micro- and macro-levels of analysis. In K. Knorr-Cetina and A. V. Cicourel (eds), *Advances in Social Theory and Methodology*. Boston and London: Routledge & Kegan Paul.

Cochran, J. (1980) When the principal is a woman. ERIC microfiche ED 184–247.

Cole, M. (1985) 'The tender trap?' Commitment and consciousness in entrants to teaching. In S. J. Ball and I. F. Goodson (eds), *Teachers' Lives and Careers*. Lewes: Falmer Press.

Collins, R. (1975) *Conflict Sociology: Towards an Explanatory Science*. New York: Academic Press.

Collins, R. (1981) Micro-translation as a theory-building strategy. In K. Knorr-Cetina and A. V. Cicourel (eds), *Advances in Social Theory and Methodology*. Boston and London: Routledge & Kegan Paul.

Cooper, C. L. and Davidson, M. (1982) *High Pressure*. London: Fontana.

Coopers & Lybrand (1989) Local management of schools. In R. Levacic (ed.), *Financial Management in Education*. Milton Keynes: Open University Press.

Corradi, C. (1991) Text, context and individual meaning: rethinking life histories in a hermeneutic framework. *Discourse and Society*, 2 (1): 105–18.

Croll, P. (1986) *Systematic Classroom Observation*. Lewes: Falmer Press.

Crow, G. (1989) The use of the concept of 'strategy' in recent sociological literative. *Sociology*, 23 (1): 1–24.

Dawe, A. (1970) The two sociologies. *British Journal of Sociology*, 21: 207–18.

Deem, R. (1978) *Women and Schooling*. London: Routledge & Kegan Paul.

Deem, R. and Wilkins, J. (1992) Governing and managing schools after ERA: the LEA experience and the GMS alternative. In T. Simkins, L. Ellison and V. Garrett (eds), *Implementing Educational Reform: The Early Lessons*. Harlow: Longman.

DeLyon, H. and Migniuolo, F. (eds) (1989) *Women Teachers: Issues and Experiences*. Milton Keynes: Open University Press.

Denzin, N. (1970) *The Research Act in Sociology*. London: Butterworth.

DES (1990) *Statistics of Education: Teachers in Service in England and Wales*. London: HMSO.

Dreeben, R. (1970) *The Nature of Teaching: School and the Work of Teachers*. Glenview, IL: Scott, Foresman.

Eagly, A. H. (1987) *Sex Differences in Social Behaviour: A Social Role Interpretation*. Hillsdale, NJ: Lawrence Erlbaum.

Earley, P. and Weindling, D. (1987) *Secondary Headship: The First Years*. Windsor, NFER-Nelson.

Earley, P. and Weindling, D. (1988) Heading for the top: the career paths of secondary school heads. *Educational Management and Administration*, 16 (1): 3–14.

Etzioni, A. (1969) (ed.) *The Semi-Professions and Their Organization: Teachers, Nurses and Social Workers*. New York: Free Press.

Evans, P. and Bartolome, F. (1980) *Must Success Cost So Much*. London: Grant McIntyre.

Evetts, J. (1990) *Women in Primary Teaching*. London: Unwin Hyman.

Evetts, J. (1991) The experiences of secondary headship selection: continuity and change. *Educational Studies*, 17 (3): 285–94.

Evetts, J. (1992) Dimensions of career: avoiding reification in the analysis of change. *Sociology*, 26: 1–21.

Evetts, J. (1994) *Women and Career: Themes and Issues in Advanced Industrial Societies*. London: Longman.

Faraday, A. and Plummer, K. (1979) Doing life histories. *Sociological Review*, 27 (4): 773–93.

Finch, J. (1983) *Married to the Job*. London: Allen & Unwin.

Floud, J. and Scott, W. (1961) Recruitment to teaching in England and Wales. In A. H. Halsey, J. Floud and C. A. Anderson (eds), *Education, Economy and Society*. New York: Free Press.

Foucault, M. (1980) *Power/Knowledge*. Brighton: Harvester.

Free, R. (1984) Study of form. In *Times Educational Supplement* 17.2.84, p. 19.

Fullan, M. (1992) *What's Worth Fighting For in Headship*? Buckingham. Open University Press.

Giddens, A. (1981) Agency, institution and time-space analysis. In K. Knorr-Cetina and A. V. Cicourel (eds), *Advances in Social Theory and Methodology*. Boston and London: Routledge & Kegan Paul.

Giddens, A. (1984) *The Constitution of Society*. Cambridge: Polity Press.

Gillborn, D. A. (1989) Talking heads: reflections on secondary headship at a time of rapid educational change. *School Organisation*, 9 (1): 65–83.

Ginsburg, M. B., Meyenn, R. J. and Miller, H. D. R. (1980) Teachers' conceptions of professionalism and trades unionism: an ideological analysis. In P. Woods (ed.), *Teacher Strategies*. London: Croom Helm.

Glaser, B. and Strauss, A. (1967) *The Discovery of Grounded Theory*. London: Weidenfeld & Nicolson.

Glazer, P. N. and Slater, M. (1987) *Unequal Colleagues: The Entrance of Women into the Professions 1890–1940*. New Brunswick, NJ: Rutgers University Press.

Glenday, N. and Price, M. (1974) *Reluctant Revolutionaries: A Century of Headmistresses 1874–1974*. London: Pitman.

Goffman, E. (1968) *Asylums*. Harmondsworth: Penguin.

Goffman, E. (1970) *Strategic Interaction*. Oxford: Basil Blackwell.

Goffman, E. (1971) *The Presentation of Self in Everyday Life*. Harmondsworth: Penguin.

Goodson, I. (1981) Life histories and the study of schooling. *Interchange* (Canada), 11 (4): 62–76.

Goodson, I. (1983) The use of life histories in the study of teaching. In M. Hammersley (ed.), *The Ethnography of Schooling*. Driffield: Nafferton.

Goodson, I. (1991) Teachers' lives and educational research. In I. Goodson and R. Walker (eds), *Biography, Identity and Schooling: Episodes in Educational Research*. Lewes: Falmer Press.

Gowler, D. and Legge, K. (1982) Dual worker families. In R. Rapoport, M. Fogarty and R. N. Rapoport (eds), *Families in Britain*. London: Routledge & Kegan Paul.

Gray, H. L. (1987) Gender considerations in school management. *School Organisation*, 7 (3): 297–302.

Greenfield, W. (1982) Research on public school principals: a review and recommendations. Paper presented at the National Conference on the Principalship convened by the National Institute of Education, October.

Gretton, J. and Jackson, M. (1976) *William Tyndale: Collapse of a School or a System?* London: Allen & Unwin.

Gunz, H. (1989) The dual meaning of managerial careers: organizational and individual levels of analysis. *Journal of Management Studies*, 26: 225–50.

Haigh, G. (1992) The heads who mind their own business. *Independent* 29.10.92, p. 18.

Hall, V., Mackay, H. and Morgan, C. (1986) *Head Teachers at Work*. Milton Keynes: Open University Press.

Hammersley, M. (1977) Teacher perspectives, Units 9/10, Course E202: *Schooling and Society*. Milton Keynes: Open University.

Hanson, D. and Herrington, M. (1976) *From College to Classroom*. London: Routledge & Kegan Paul.

Harré, R. (1981) Philosophical aspects of the micro-macro problem. In K. Knorr-Cetina and A. V. Cicourel (eds), *Advances in Social Theory and Methodology*. Boston and London: Routledge & Kegan Paul.

Hill, D., Oakley Smith, B. and Spinks, J. (1990) *Local Management of Schools*. London: Paul Chapman.

Hilsum, S. and Start, K. B. (1974) *Promotion and Careers in Teaching*. Slough: NFER.

Hoffman, N. (1981) *Women's 'True' Profession*. Old Westbury, NY: Feminist Press.

Homans, G. (1964) Bringing men back in. *American Sociological Review*, 29: 809–18.

Houghton, V., McHugh, R. and Morgan, C. (eds) (1975) *Management in Education*. London: Ward Lock.

Hoyle, E. (1975) The study of schools as organizations. In V. Houghton, R. McHugh and C. Morgan (eds), *Management in Education: Reader 1*. London: Ward Lock.

Hoyle, E. (1981) The process of management. In *Management and the School*, E323 Block 3. Milton Keynes: Open University.

Hoyle, E. (1982) Micropolitics of educational organizations. *Educational Management and Administration*, 10: 87–98.

Hoyle, E. (1986) *The Politics of School Management*. London: Hodder & Stoughton.

Hughes, E. C. (1937) Institutional office and the person. *American Journal of Sociology*, 43: 404–13.

Hughes, E. C. (1958) *Men and Their Work*. Glencoe, IL: Free Press.

Hughes, M. C. (1972) The role of the secondary head. PhD thesis, University of Wales.

Hughes, M. (1986) Theory and practice in educational management. In M. Hughes, P. Ribbins and H. Thomas (eds), *Managing Education: The System and the Institution*. London: Holt, Rinehart & Winston.

Hunt, J. W. (1986, 2nd ed.) *Managing People at Work*. London: McGraw-Hill.

Kanter, R. M. (1977) *Men and Women of the Corporation*. New York: Basic Books.

Kaufman, P. W. (1984) *Women Teachers on the Frontier*. New Haven, CT: Yale University Press.

Kavanagh, D. (1987) *Thatcherism and British Politics*. Oxford: Oxford University Press.

Kelsall, R. K. (1963) *Women and Teaching*. Sheffield: Sheffield University Press.

King, R. (1983) *The Sociology of School Organizations*. London: Methuen.

Knorr-Cetina, K. and Cicourel, A. V. (eds) (1981) *Advances in Social Theory and Methodology*. Boston and London: Routledge & Kegan Paul.

Lacey, C. (1977) *The Socialization of Teachers*. London: Methuen.

Lawn, M. and Ozga, J. (1981) *Teachers, Professionalism and Class*. Lewes: Falmer Press.

Lawn, M. and Grace, G. (eds) (1987) *Teachers: The Culture and Politics of Work*. Lewes: Falmer Press.

Leggatt, T. (1970) Teaching as a profession. In J. A. Jackson (ed.), *Professions and Professionalization*. Cambridge: Cambridge University Press.

Levacic, R. (ed.) (1989) *Financial Management in Education*. Milton Keynes: Open University Press.

Lieberman, M. (1956) *Education as a Profession*. Englewood Cliffs, NJ: Prentice-Hall.

Lortie, D. (1975) *School-teacher: A Sociological Study*. Chicago: University of Chicago Press.

Lyons, G. (1974) *The Administrative Tasks of Head and Senior Teachers in Large Secondary Schools*. Bristol: University of Bristol, School of Education Research Unit.

Lyons, G. (1976) *Heads' Tasks: A Handbook of Secondary School Administration*. Slough: NFER.

Lyons, G. (1981) *Teacher Careers and Career Perceptions*. Windsor: NFER-Nelson.

Lyons, G. and Stenning, R. (1986) *Managing Staff in Schools: A Handbook*. London: Hutchinson.

MacKenzie, R. F. (1977) *The Unbowed Head*. Edinburgh: Edinburgh University Press.

Marshall, J. (1984) *Women Managers*. Chichester: Wiley.

Marwick, A. (1982) *British Society Since 1945*. Harmondsworth: Penguin.

McCleary, L. and Thomson, S. (1979) *The Senior High School Principalship*. Reston, VA: NASSP.

McCrone, D., Elliott, B. and Bechhofer, F. (1989) Corporation and the New Right. In R. Scase (ed.), *Industrial Societies*. London: Allen & Unwin.

McRae, S. (1986) *Cross-Class Families: A Study of Wives' Occupational Superiority*. Oxford: Clarendon Press.

Measor, L. (1985) Critical incidents in the classroom: identities, choices and careers. In S. J. Ball and I. F. Goodson (eds), *Teachers' Lives and Careers*. Lewes: Falmer Press.

Mitchell, J. C. (1983) Case and situation analysis. *Sociological Review*, 31: 187–211.

Morgan, C., Hall, V. and Mackay, H. (1983) *The Selection of Secondary School Headteachers*. Milton Keynes: Open University Press.

Morgan, D. H. J. (1989) Strategies and sociologists: a comment on Crow. *Sociology*, 23 (1): 25–9.

Morgan, G. (1986) *Images of Organization*. London: Sage.

National Foundation for Educational Research (1989) *The Recruitment, Retention, Motivation and Morale of Senior Staff in Schools*. Slough: NFER.

Nias, J. (1984) The definition and maintenance of self in primary teaching. *British Journal of Sociology of Education*, 5 (3): 167–80.

Nias, J. (1985) Reference groups in primary teaching. In S. Ball and F. Goodson (eds), *Teachers' Lives and Careers*. Lewes: Falmer Press.

Nicholson, N. and West, M. (1988) *Managerial Job Change*. Cambridge: Cambridge University Press.

O'Leary, V. E. and Ickovics, J. R. (1992) Cracking the glass ceiling. In U. Sekaran and F. T. L. Leong (eds), *Womanpower*. Newbury Park, CA: Sage.

Oram, A. (1983) Serving two masters? The introduction of a marriage bar in teaching in the 1920s. In London Feminist History Group (eds), *The Sexual Dynamics of History*. London: Pluto Press.

Oram, A. (1985) 'Sex antagonism' in the teaching profession: the equal pay issue 1914–1929. *History of Education Review* (Australia), 14 (1): 36–48.

Oram, A. (1987) 'Sex antagonism' in the teaching profession: equal pay and the marriage bar 1910–39. In M. Arnot and G. Weiner (eds), *Gender and the Politics of Schooling*. London: Hutchinson.

Ostell, A. and Oakland, S. (1993) *Headteacher Stress, Coping and Health*. Bradford: University of Bradford, Management Centre.

Owen, P. (1985) Application for headship. *Education Management and Administration*, 13 (1): 45–9.

Ozga, J. (1981) The politics of the teaching profession. Open University Course E353: *Society Education and the State*. Milton Keynes: Open University.

Ozga, J. (1992) (ed.) *Women in Educational Management*. Buckingham: Open University Press.

Pahl, R. E. (1984) *Divisions of Labour*. Oxford: Blackwell.

Partington, G. (1976) *Women Teachers in the Twentieth Century in England and Wales*. Slough: NFER.

Peters, R. S. (ed) (1976) *The Role of the Head*. London: Routledge & Kegan Paul.

Plummer, K. (1975) *Sexual Stigma*. London: Routledge & Kegan Paul.

Plummer, K. (1983) *Documents of Life*. London: Allen & Unwin.

Purvis, J. (1973) Schoolteaching as a professional career. *British Journal of Sociology*, 24 (1): 43–57.

Rapoport, R. and Rapoport, R. N. (1971) *Dual-Career Families*. Harmondsworth: Penguin.

Rapoport, R. and Rapoport, R. N. (1976) *Dual-Career Families Re-examined*. Oxford: Martin · Robertson.

Rapoport, R. and Rapoport R. N. (1978) (eds) *Working Couples*. London: Routledge & Kegan Paul.

Rapoport, R. and Sierakowski, M. (1982) *Recent Social Trends in Family and Work in Britain*. London: Institute of Family and Environmental Research/Policy Studies Institute.

Richards, C. (1987) Primary education in England. In S. Delamont (ed.), *The Primary School Teacher*. Lewes: Falmer Press.

Riseborough, G. (1981) Teacher careers and comprehensive schooling. *Sociology*, 15 (3): 352–81.

Riseborough, G. (1985) Pupils, teachers' careers and schooling: an empirical study. In S. J. Ball and I. F. Goodson (eds), *Teachers' Lives and Careers*. Lewes: Falmer Press.

Robertson, J. (1985) *Future Work*. Aldershot: Gower/Temple Smith.

Roethlisberger, F. J. and Dickson, W. J. (1939) *Management and the Worker*. Cambridge, MA: Harvard University Press.

Salaman, G. (1974) *Community and Occupation*. Cambridge: Cambridge University Press.

Saran, R. and Verber, L. (1979) The Burnham unit total system. *Educational Administration*, 8 (1): 113–37.

Scase, R. and Goffee, R. (1989) *Reluctant Managers*. London: Unwin Hyman.

Scott, J. (1986) Gender: A useful category of historical analysis. *American Historical Review*, 91: 1053–75.

Scott, R. (1964) *The Making of Blind Men*. New York: Sage.

Shakeshaft, C. (1979) Dissertation research on women in educational administration: a synthesis of findings and paradigm for future research. *Dissertation Abstracts International*, 40: 6455a.

Shakeshaft, C. (1985) Strategies for overcoming the barriers to women in educational administration. In S. Klein (ed.), *Handbook for Achieving Sexual Equity Through Education*. Baltimore: Johns Hopkins University Press.

Shakeshaft, C. (1987) *Women in Educational Administration*. Beverly Hills and London: Sage.

Sharp, R. and Green, A. (1975) *Education and Social Control*. London: Routledge & Kegan Paul.

Sikes, P. (1985) The life cycle of the teacher. In S. J. Ball and I. F. Goodson (eds), *Teachers' Lives and Careers*. Lewes: Falmer Press.

Sikes, P., Measor, L. and Woods, P. (1985) *Teacher Careers*. Lewes: Falmer Press.

Simkins, T., Ellison, L. and Garrett, V. (1992) Beyond markets and managerialism? Education management in a new context. In T. Simkins *et al.* (eds), *Implementing Educational Reform: The Early Lessons*. Harlow: Longman.

Simpson, R. L. and Simpson, I. H. (1969) Women and bureaucracy in the semi-professions. In

A. Etzioni (ed.), *The Semi-Professions and their Organization: Teachers, Nurses and Social Workers*. New York: Free Press.

Smith, D. (1975) Career structure of headteachers in a Midlands city. *Educational Review*, 28: 31–41.

Smith, L. M., Klein, P. F., Dwyer, D. C., and Prunty, J. J. (1985) Educational innovators: a decade and a half late later. In S. J. Ball and I. F. Goodson (eds), *Teachers' Lives and Careers*. Lewes: Falmer Press.

Spencer, A. (1986) Gender in the labour process – the case of women and men lawyers. In D. Knights and H. Willmott (eds), *Gender and the Labour Process*. London: Gower.

Stebbins, R. A. (1970) Careers: the subjective approach. *Sociological Quarterly*, pp. 32–49.

Stewart, J. (1986) *The New Management of Local Government*. London: Allen & Unwin.

Stiles, L. J. (ed) (1957) *The Teacher's Role in American Society*. New York: Harper & Row.

Strauss, A. L. (1977) *Mirrors and Masks: The Search for Identity*. London: Martin Robertson.

Taylor, J. K. and Dale, I. R. (1971) *A Survey of Teachers in their First Year of Service*. Bristol: University of Bristol, School of Education Research Unit.

Taylor, L. and Cohen, S. (1972) *Psychological Survival*. Harmondsworth: Penguin.

Tropp, A. (1957) *The School Teachers*. London: Heinemann.

Turner, C. M. (1968) An organizational analysis of a secondary modern school. *Sociological Review*, 17 (1): 67–87.

Turner, R. H. (1962) 'Role making': process versus conformity. In A. M. Rose (ed.), *Human Behaviour and Social Processes: An Interactionist Approach*. Boston: Houghton Mifflin.

Vansina, J. (1985) *Oral Tradition as History*. London: James Currey.

West-Burnham, J. (1983) A discussion of the implications for secondary school management of a static career structure. *School Organization*, 3 (3): 255–62.

Widdowson, F. (1980) *Going Up into the Next Class*. London: WRRC Publications.

Wilce, H. (1989) When the head means business. *Independent* 14.12.89, p. 19.

Wilson, B. (1962) The teacher's role: a sociological analysis. In *British Journal of Sociology*, 3 (1): 15–32.

Winkley, D. (1985) *Diplomats and Detectives: LEA Advisers at Work*. London: Robert Royce.

Wolcott, H. (1973) *The Man in the Principal's Office*. New York: Holt, Rinehart & Winston.

Woods, P. (1979) *The Divided School*. London: Routledge & Kegan Paul.

Woods, P. (1980) *Teacher Strategies*. London: Croom Helm.

Woods, P. (1981) Strategies, commitment and identity: making and speaking the teacher role. In L. Barton and S. Walker (eds), *Schools, Teachers and Teaching*. Lewes: Falmer Press.

Woods, P. (1983) *Sociology and the School: An Interactionist Viewpoint*. London: Routledge & Kegan Paul.

Woods, P. (1985) Conversations with teachers. *British Educational Research Journal*, 11 (1): 13–26.

Wrong, D. (1961) The oversocialized conception of man in modern sociology. *American Sociological Review*, 26: 183–93.

Young, M. and Willmott, P. (1973) *The Symmetrical Family*. London: Routledge & Kegan Paul.

Name Index

Abrams, P.   8, 12, 13, 49
Acker, S.   2, 40, 50, 85, 94, 121
Adams, N.   1, 69
Adkison, J.   3, 87
Allan, G.   48
Allen, B.   2
Apple, M. W.   121
Archer, J.   88
Atkinson, P.   12
Auld, R.   2

Ball, S. J.   1, 2, 3, 4, 6, 14, 16, 20, 50, 57,
    70, 71, 85, 86, 88, 89, 94
Barry, C. H.   2
Bartolome, F.   50
Bechhofer, F.   120
Becker, H. S.   12
Bennet, C.   19, 21
Berg, L.   2
Berger, P. L.   12
Bertaux, D.   7
Beynon, J.   7-8, 26
Blumberg, A.   1
Bott, E.   48
Bourdieu, P.   52
Burgess, R. G.   2-3, 7, 12, 26, 27, 71, 88,
    121
Bush, T.   1, 69, 71
Byrne, E.   2

Callon, M.   24
Chapman, J. B.   85
Cicourel, A. V.   14, 22, 23
Clegg, Sir Alec   44
Cochran, J.   3, 87
Cohen, S.   9
Cole, M.   26
Collins, R.   14, 48
Cooper, C. L.   50
Coopers & Lybrand   18
Corradi, C.   7
Croll, P.   7
Crow, G.   9, 10, 51, 52, 67-8

Dale, I. R.   89
Davidson, M.   50
Deem, R.   2, 18
Delamont, S.   12

DeLyon, H.   2
Denzin, N.   7
DES   3, 85
Dickson, W. J.   20
Dreeben, R.   26
Dwyer, D. C.   7

Eagly, A. H.   93, 94
Earley, P.   1, 2, 3, 4, 20, 88, 95, 107
Elliott, B.   120
Ellison, L.   121
Etzioni, A.   1
Evans, P.   50
Evetts, J.   1, 2, 5, 10, 14, 18, 47-8, 107,
    121

Faraday, A.   7
Finch, J.   57
Floud, J.   1, 2
Foucault, M.   67
Free, R.   40
Fullan, M.   2, 107

Garrett, V.   121
Geer, B.   12
Giddens, A.   14, 21-2, 25, 49, 104-5
Gillborn, D. A.   3, 88, 121
Gilligan, C.   12
Ginsburg, M. B.   27
Glaser, B.   5
Glazer, P. N.   10
Glenday, N.   2
Goffee, R.   20, 50, 120
Goffman, E.   9, 89
Goodson, I.   1, 2, 6, 7, 14, 16, 20
Gowler, D.   50, 57
Grace, G.   15, 121
Gray, H. L.   88
Green, A.   2
Greenfield, W.   1
Gretton, J.   2
Gunz, H.   14, 104, 105

Haigh, G.   18
Hall, V.   3, 4, 40, 88, 107
Hammersley, M.   2, 26
Hanson, D.   89
Harre   21

Subject Index

advisers 100, 105
allowances 19, 26, 31, 72-3, 74, 120-1
    distribution of 74, 76-8, 81-2, 83
    fixing of 80
    local education authorities and 74
    reduction in 75
authority
    collegial model 70
    hierarchical model 70, 74
    and organization theory 70
    and school micro-politics 111

budgets
    devolution of 5, 17-18, 107-8
    governors' responsibilities 17, 18
    and grant-maintained status 17-18
Burnham Scale 19, 72, 73

career action 14, 20-1, 95-6, 107, 120-2
    analysing change in 22-5
    and structure 21-2
career development, after headship 95-106
career development, *see also* promotion
career history approach 8-9
career maps 27
career and salary structures 15, 19-20
    Basic Scale 72
    Burnham scale 19, 72, 73
    effect of local financial management on
      20
    elaboration of 95
    flexibility within 102-3
    for headteachers 101-3
    Incentive Allowances, *see* allowances
    and legislative change 105-6
    and management 72-5
    modification of 13, 22-3, 60-1, 72
    and pay disputes 15
    and powers of headteachers 71, 72-84
careers
    changing research models 14
    commitment to 7, 33-4, 37-8, 104
    dialectical nature of 6-7
    dual, *see* dual career families
    expectations of 104
    gender differences in, *see* gender
    'interrupted' 19, 36-7
    jobs changing into 23

local, regional and national interactions
    24
objective and subjective dimensions
    6-7, 20-3
as process 11, 50-1
public and private elements of 13,
    19-20
and short-term thinking 10
single 50, 52-3, 54-7
structures and action 14-20, 21-5,
    95-6, 104-5, 120-2
closure of schools 15
collective action 21, 22
    and career patterns 105
    household strategies 52
commitment, to teaching as career 7, 33-4,
    37-8, 104
community education 76
comprehensive schools
    difficulties during reorganization 28-9
    rise of 1, 27-33, 59, 75
concerns of headteachers 99-106
conflict
    and leadership styles 87
    and single career strategies 57
convenience 34-5, 38
curricular responsibilities 6, 26, 27, 29
cutbacks in spending 15-16

demographic changes 14-15
    and gender 16
discrimination 39, 43, 90, 93
dual career families 50, 53, 57-64
    balancing strategies 58, 61-4, 66, 67
    modification strategies 57-8, 60-1, 64,
      66-7
    postponement strategies 57, 58-60, 63,
      64, 66
    problems of wife's success 61-4, 65-6

Education Acts
    (1944) 28
    (1986) 18
    (1987) 75
    (1993) 17
    Education Reform Act (1988) 17, 18,
      75, 121
empty-nest syndrome 55-6

examination results 32, 59
experimentation 15

family responsibilities 34-7
  and career satisfaction 97-9
  and career strategies 11, 13, 51-68
  gender differences 54-68
  research into 50-1
feminism 90-1
formula funding 107-8, 121
  maintenance and running costs 114-16
Funding Agency 17

gender 13
  and attitudes of governors 43, 90
  and career concerns 97-9, 100-1
  and career strategies 9-11
  and demographic changes 16
  differences in early and mid career 31, 33-8
  and discrimination 39, 42-3, 90
  and experience of headship 89-94
  historicization of 12
  and leadership styles 3-4, 86-9, 121-2
  and management 85-6
  and marginalization 3, 85
  and pastoral responsibilities 39, 78-9, 81
  and promotion 35-9, 48
  research on 2, 3-4
  stereotypes 88-9, 93-4
governors 3, 107
  and gender discrimination 43, 90
  relationship with headteachers 111, 112-13
  responsibilities of 5, 17, 18
  and school micro-politics 111-13
  and selection of headteachers 40, 43-4
  and staffing levels 110
  sub-committees 111-13
grammar schools 28-32
grant-maintained status (GMS) 1, 13, 16, 17-18, 105, 107
grant-maintained status (GMS)
  advantages of 17-18
  Funding Agency 17
  and status of teachers 121

heads of department 26, 27, 29
house systems 26, 27

identity
  historical formation of 12-13
  and personal experience 12
  and structure 12, 49
income generation by headteachers 116-18
infant schools 3, 5, 85
inspectors 42-3, 48, 100, 105
interactionist perspective in research 2, 3, 6-9, 21-3
  concept of strategy 9
  and personal identity 12
  and work roles 89
interview procedures 44-7
isolation 118-19

leadership styles 3, 90, 94
  charismatic 97, 99
  definition 86
  democratic 87
  and gender 3-4, 86-9
  ideal-type categories 4, 88
  masculine and feminine 87-9
  research into 87-8
LEAs (local education authorities) 3, 38, 96
  and development of comprehensive schools 28
  and grant-maintained status 17-18
  officials 107
  and promotion allowances 74
  and selection of headteachers 40-1, 43-4, 48
legislative change 15, 46
  and role of headteachers 107
  and salary and career structure 105-6
leisure interests 98-9
length in post 5-6
life-history approach, advantages of 7-8
LMS (local financial management) 1, 5, 16-17, 46, 69, 75, 96, 98, 105
  budgetary devolution 1, 5
  effects on headteachers 13, 17, 18
  formula funding 107-8, 114-16
  and income generation 116-18
  local variations in 17
  maintenance and running costs 114-16
  and micro-political activities 108-11
  and role of new headteacher 118-19
  and salary structure 20
  and staffing levels 108-11
  and status of teachers 121
location of schools 6

maintenance and running costs 114-16
management
  assessment of in selection of headteachers 46-7
  career and salary structures and 13, 72-5
  changing role of headteachers 1
  and cultural contradictions 85-6, 121-2
  and educational change 72, 75-8
  and gender 3, 85-6
  hierarchical model 1, 27, 79-80, 84
  influence of theory on 69-71
  masculine style of 86
  measurement of performance 121
  research into 69
  systems of 73-5
  transfer of skills 102-3
  underrepresentation of women 85, *see also* LMS (local financial management)
management plans 17
marginalization, and gender 3, 85
marital breakdown 53, 64-6, 67